Don't Invest and Forget

Don't Invest and Forget

A look at the importance of
having a comprehensive,
dynamic investment plan

Pat Vitucci

To order additional copies of this book, contact:
Xlibris Corporation
1-888-795-4274
www.Xlibris.com
Orders@Xlibris.com
27461

Contents

I dedicate this book to:

* Teresa Newkirk—whose tireless help was invaluable in the preparation of the book.

* My wife, Elaine, and my son, Jason,—for their wonderful support and encouragement.

* My staff—without whom all of this would not be possible.

1

Understanding Market Risk

Money frees you from doing things you dislike. Since I dislike
doing nearly everything, money is handy.—Groucho Marx

Chances are you're interested in achieving a financial goal that will involve investing in order to fulfill your dream. Whether it is being able to easily afford an Ivy League education for your children or a comfortable retirement for yourself, we all have goals that we realize will need careful planning and investing to achieve. It's very important to not only plan ahead for your financial future, but to carefully evaluate which investments you choose. So to begin, let's take a look at market risk.

Simply stated, when the stock market declines, it tends to pull down most stocks with it. This is market risk. Stocks and most other investments are affected by market risk. We've all heard fabulous stories of lucky people who have invested a small amount of money in an unknown company and are now extremely wealthy thanks to that tiny investment. Likewise, there are countless stories of unlucky people who have eagerly placed their hard-earned dollars into the market and now have nothing to show for all their hard work.

Warren Buffett, one of the most thriving investors and one of the world's wealthiest men, commented in Harry Dent's book, *The Warren Buffett Way*, "To be successful, one needs good business judgment and the ability to protect oneself from the emotional whirlwind that the market unleashes." Buffett believes, "investors must be financially and psychologically prepared to deal with the market volatility. Investors should expect their common stocks to fluctuate. Unless you can watch your stock holdings decline by 50% without becoming panic-stricken, you should not be in the stock market." (p.184)

One way to hopefully avoid disaster is to first gain a clear understanding of the risks involved with investing. As with any financial decision, the better educated you are about where your money is going—the better off you will be. Entering the market is no different. Let's take a look at specific types of market risks that are out there and then you can decide which ones are right for your peace of mind. Please keep in mind: no investment is worth losing sleep over, regardless of the potential gains.

Investments offer a complete spectrum of risks, from very low risks (such as a CD or money market account[1]) to very high risks (such as individual company stocks.) Naturally, the lower the risk is the lower the expected returns will be on your money, and vice versa. There are a number of other risks involved with investing. You need to understand what factors can affect your investments so that you are able to choose the right investment for your financial goals.

---

[1]   An investment in the Fund is not insured or guaranteed by the Federal Deposit Insurance Corporation or any other government agency. Although the Fund seeks to preserve the value of your investment at $1.00 per share, it is possible to lose money by investing in the Fund.

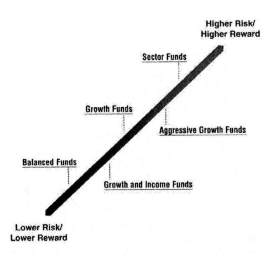

Some investments are subject to *inflation risk*. Some alternatives such as savings accounts may fail to outpace inflation[2]. If the rate of inflation is higher than the return on your investments, they may actually lose purchasing power over time. Yes, your money is very safely tucked away in the bank vault, but it isn't likely to grow over time at a high rate. So you're in fact losing money in the long term by not allowing it to grow. Savings accounts are ideal for immediate money reserves and contingency funds, but not for your retirement fund. Other investments are subject to *interest rate risk*. The value of a bond falls if interest rates rise. If you buy a bond at 3% and interest rates rise, new bonds will be offered at higher rates. If you need to sell your bond before it matures, you'll have to sell it at a discount. Once again, your money is in a safe investment (U.S. Treasury bonds are backed by the full faith and credit of the U.S. government[3]) but this money is still not going to grow at a desirable rate. Ironically, some people feel safe keeping much of their money in low yielding Treasury bonds

---

[2]   CDs and savings accounts are FDIC insured.

[3]   U.S. Treasury bonds are backed by the full faith and credit of the U.S. Government if held to maturity.

issued by the U.S. Government. Lending your money to the government has some patriotic value, but it certainly is not 100% risk free.

> Just as Inflation Increases Everyday Costs
> Likewise, Your Investments Need to Keep Pace

Fig. 3: Everyday Items Will Cost More

	Price Today	Price 20 Years From Now
A pair of jeans	$35	$63
A new car	$15,000	$27,092
A new house	$120,000	$216,733

Assumes 4% inflation. Prices may vary by location.

Some stock investments are subject to *economic risk*. We've seen plenty examples of this exact situation recently. As you remember, following September 11, 2001, many companies faced severe economic hardships. This resulted in a complete domino effect: loss of jobs, downturn in the stock market, lowered inflation and many other elements to a downturn in the economic cycle. Even after the stock market began to regain its momentum, the tide did not turn quickly. One of the overpowering effects of economic risk is that it can have such a big impact on so many different industries. Some large companies are especially vulnerable to changes in economic conditions. Automakers, airlines, technology, and various others suffered more with the onset of a recession than manufacturers of consumer goods. However, this was a natural occurrence with today's world economy. We can all be impacted by what not only happens in our country, but also by the political and economic twists and turns in other areas around the globe.

There will always be periods of upswings and downturns in the stock market, which is why investors must always be thinking long-term.

Long-term investing, that is the length of time you have to reach your goal, will help you choose appropriate investments. With time on your side, you may be able to take bigger risks in order to take advantage of greater potential returns. A 25-year old investor will definitely be discouraged by a sharp drop in the economy; but a 75-year old investor could be devastated. The 25-year old has the element of time on her side to recover losses, while the 75-year old might not enjoy the luxury of time to recover his losses. So when you consider your investments, you must always take into account what type of risks you are willing to consider and at what level. This involves assessing your own personal appetite for risk.

There are an incredible amount of issues that affect the market's performance. The following list is but a small sampling:

- The Federal Reserve's monetary policy
- Inflation Rate
- Housing Starts
- Manufacturing Index
- Consumer Price Index
- Gross Domestic Product
- Sentiment Indicators
- Consumer Confidence Index
- Blue Chip Index
- Unemployment Numbers
- The Political Climate

It is the combination of these and several hundred other indices, sprinkled with the emotions of the day throughout the globe, which dictates whether the markets will rise or fall.

Your individual portfolio should maintain a diversified approach utilizing a variety of the segments of the economy that behave very differently based on current conditions. Listed below are several components that could make up a portfolio (certainly the make-up of any one portfolio is based upon the risk tolerance and goals of the individual):

- Large Company Stocks
- Small Company Stocks
- Mid-Size Company Stocks
- Growth Company Stocks
- Value Company Stocks
- Corporate Bonds
- Utilities
- Real Estate
- U.S. Government Securities
- Emerging Markets
- Cash
- International Markets
- Global Markets

All investments carry risk. As with your day-to-day life, some risks are much more apparent than others. One of the best ways to reduce investment risk is to "buy" yourself some "insurance" via diversification[4]. Diversification simply means that you place your investment dollars into various investments that perform differently under particular economic circumstances. People who worry a lot may easily justify diversifying since they can easily dream up possible calamities.

While the stock market is more volatile in the short-term than the bond market, stock market investors have earned far better long-term returns than do bond investors[1]. Remember that bonds will generally outperform keeping your hard-earned nickels in a boring old bank account. The risk of a stock or bond market

---

[4]   Diversification does not ensure against loss.

[1]   Past performance is not a guarantee of future results.

fall becomes less of a concern the longer the time period you plan to invest. In fact, over any 20-year period, the U.S. stock market investors have never lost money, even after subtracting for the effects of inflation[5].

Skittish investors may desire to keep all their money in bonds and money market[6] accounts. The risk in this strategy is that your money will not grow enough over the years in order for you to accomplish your financial goals. In other words, the lower the return that you earn, the more you need to save to reach a goal. A 40-year old seeking to accumulate $500,000 by the age of 65 will need to save $722 per month if she earns a 6% annual return. But that same smart lady will only need to save $377 per month if she can earn a 10% annual return (this may require assuming some more risk). As Albert Einstein once said, "the two most beautiful words in the English language are compound interest." Younger investors should pay very close attention to the risk of generating low returns, but so too should the younger senior citizens. At the age of 65 in today's world, you should recognize that a portion of your assets will probably not be used for a decade or two.

Some catastrophes can be avoided by doing your homework. When you purchase real estate, a whole gamut of inspections can save you from buying a pig in a poke. With stocks, examining some measures of value and the company's financial condition and business strategy can reduce your chances of buying into an overpriced company or one on the verge of major problems. With that in mind, you can easily see one of the advantages to

---

[5]   Index used: S&P 500. Past Performance is no guarantee of future results.

[6]   An investment in the Fund is not insured or guaranteed by the Federal Deposit Insurance Corporation or any other government agency. Although the Fund seeks to preserve the value of your investment at $1.00 per share, it is possible to lose money by investing in the Fund.

investing in mutual funds. A mutual fund offers professional management and oversight as well as diversification[2].

Lessons Learned from the Dot.com Boom-Bust

The second half of the 1990's witnessed one of the most impressive periods of economic prosperity in recent economic history with low unemployment, low inflation, substantial growth in real GDP and high real wages. Many analysts impressed with the spectacular performance of the economy were moved to declare the end of the business cycle. The problem with the prosperity of the 1990's was that the period also coincided with one of the greatest financial bubbles in U.S. economy history. Share prices of technology, media, and telecommunication companies skyrocketed. Amazingly enough analysts and experts were able to convince investors that these unreal P/E ratios were actually reasonable and justifiable via the miracle of the "New Economy."

With investor's paper wealth rising at amazing rates, individuals and businesses indulged in massive borrowing and investing, and of course, there was no need to save. The age of eternal prosperity was here. Why worry? Making lots of money was easy. You could write up a business plan on the back of a napkin during lunch. Get financed by a venture capitalist, go on a spending binge for an IPO, and then cash out. It was simple, was it not? Things really did not work out after a while as ill-conceived business plans eventually meant zero results. Ideals that were supposed to change the world went to scrap heap of failure as hundreds

---

[2]   Mutual funds include additional costs such as an expense ratio and sales charge . Funds may also generate a capital gain while individual stock investors have control over the generation of a capital gain. Diversification does not ensure against loss

of dot.coms bit the dust. The bust was here. What are the lessons of this debacle?

We can obtain several lessons from the rise and fall of the dot.coms and the collapse of the stock market bubble:

Hubris is not a substitute for a well-developed business plan even when we are dealing with a brand new technology that many think will alter our future. A revolutionary technology such as the Internet requires as much planning and thought as a routine new technology. The euphoria surrounding new technologies can create such unrealistic financial expectations that sound economics and good business sense disappeared. The same important business principles of any business need to be well-thought out and applied, whether the company is on the web or on Main Street.

The dot.com debacle reminds us of past speculative episodes. These include the 17th century "Tulip Mania" in Western Europe, the 18th century South Seas Company Bubble, the Crash of 1929, and the Junk Bond Fiasco of the 1980's. The economy is subject to recurrent episodes of speculative fever, with accompanying euphoria followed by financial ruin for many.

The unique feature of the dot.com crash was that we have seldom seen such reckless financing by venture capitalists, investment bankers, and investors. It was the second Gold Rush in California and it fizzled out much faster than the first one. The telecom meltdown is a combination of highly unrealistic business expectations, as well as, serious management ethical lapses. The impacts range from fall in equity prices, loss of jobs, erosion of retirement nest eggs, and loss of confidence in our business leadership because of serious ethical malfeasance including fraudulent accounting. The obvious lesson here is that sustainable business success is only possible with prudent business planning as well as a firm stand on good business ethics.

Finally, we'd like to warn you about "rear-view investment risk." Some investors chase after investments that have recently performed strongly, assuming that the trend will continue. This is a very dangerous proposition because it often leads investors into investments that have already had their run in the market and perhaps even peaked. Maybe you've heard the old adage about buy low and sell high. Chasing after investments that have performed quite well recently can lead to buying high—not a recommended practice.

Now that we've explored several favors of risk, it's a good time to ask yourself, "what level of risk can I tolerate?" Some people can't stomach risk. Others are at a time in their lives when they can't afford to take great risk. If you're near or in retirement, your portfolio and nerves may not be able to wait a decade for your riskier investments to recover after a major stumble. Perhaps you have sufficient assets to accomplish your financial goals and are more concerned with preserving what you do have, rather than risking it to grow more.

🗀 From The Real Life Files of Pat Vitucci

The following is a real life example where the names have been changed. But the situation described is accurate.

Marilyn is a 65 year old widow who recently lost her husband to stomach cancer. John had always managed the finances and studied where to invest their portfolio. Marilyn was devastated with her loss and understandably overwhelmed with the prospects of managing her portfolio. Her best friend told her to avoid any risks on her money, and she should invest all of her portfolio in bond funds. Because her friend has been so supportive during her time of grief, her well-intended advice was readily received. Marilyn adjusted her portfolio accordingly.

Pat's Recommendation:

A 65 year old *young* female has the prospects of living approximately 20 more years. Therefore Marilyn needs to have her money outpace inflation and provide some growth of her portfolio to maintain her lifestyle. She has positioned herself to under perform the markets and has volunteered inadvertently for a significant interest rate risk. Bond markets can change quickly and swiftly without warning. The media emphasizes stock market volatility but provides very little "press time" to interest rate fluctuations. Marilyn's best friend was well intentioned, but Marilyn should consider enrolling in continuing educational courses on personal finance management and immediately seek counsel from a financial professional. We would also urge Marilyn to first read Chapter 8 on "Selection of a Financial Advisor."

Key Points from Chapter 1:

1. There are several types of risk associated with investing and each investor needs to have a clear understanding of them.
2. By diversifying your investment choices you can offset many of the downsides to risk.
3. Be sure that the risks you take are in alignment with your overall financial picture.

2

Your Personal Appetite for Risk

Money was never a big motivation for me, except as a way to keep score. The real excitement is playing the game.—Donald Trump

Many of us spent hours of our childhood playing the board game RISK and whether or not you won usually depended upon your willingness to take chances and a little bit of luck. Risk is simply the measurement of how willing you are to see the value of your investments decrease in the near term, even while you know the chances that they will increase over the long term. The higher the risk is in an investment, the more likely it is to drop in the short term as well as to rise.

When the financial markets suffer earthshaking events, some investors worry that their investments are in shambles. As with earthquakes, the media is often to blame because of its hyping short-term events and blowing them out of proportion to entice viewers and listeners. History has shown that financial markets recover; it's just a question of time. If you're in investments for the longer-term, then the last six weeks—or even last couple of years—is a short time period. And a mountain of evidence and studies demonstrate that no one can predict the future, so there's little use in your trying to base your investment plans on predictions.

A big danger that larger-than-normal market declines hold is that they may encourage decision-making based on emotion rather than logic. Just ask anyone who was in the market during the beginning of the 2000's. Stock market declines, like earthquakes, bring all sorts of prognosticators and gurus out of the woodwork. This is especially true in the financial world. Today's consumer of personal finance information faces overload. You can't pick up a newspaper or magazine or any other media outlet without bumping into articles and advice columns devoted to personal finance.

Some of the biggest mistakes many investors make are emotional ones. When our stocks are going up, we tend to throw caution to the winds in our pursuit of ever greater profits. Likewise, when our stocks are dropping, we tend to panic and dump otherwise sound investments, because we're afraid of ever greater losses. When is the "right" time to sell or buy? Prudent investors have learned through experience to temper their emotional reactions, but low volatility in a stock can make patient and disciplined investors of us all.

But we'd like to encourage you to take inventory and see what "feels right for you" rather than following the latest hot pick. A big portion of determining that will be to decide what level of personal investment risk is comfortable for you. Two people can be the same age, live in similar homes, and even have the same career, yet one will be a very aggressive investor and sleep easily at night—while the other will invest rather conservatively so that he too can sleep easily. It boils down to choosing what feels right for you and your situation.

In modern finance, risk is defined as the variability of returns. If an investment's value climbs up and down quite a bit, it is deemed to be riskier than an investment that stays put or climbs slowly—even if the one that jumps around a lot tends to outperform the slower moving investment over time. When your returns are more variable, you have more of a chance to lose money. When looking at the returns of equity investments over history, stocks typically outperform all other investments over long periods of time. In any 10 year period, if you invested in stocks, you have a 90%+ opportunity to outperform anything else[1].

Risk does sound like a pretty serious problem. So how do you go about identifying your risk tolerance? Before you start buying, you need to assess how much risk you are willing to accept and then select investments based on that risk tolerance level. This, in part, can be determined by your investment time frame or, estimating when you will need the money.

If you look at the long-term historical returns that investment vehicles like stocks have generated, you probably have second thoughts about sticking with the low-risk, low-return vehicles that serve as safe havens for money. For example: from 1950 to 1995 an investor would have earned a total return of 19,300% in stocks versus 523% in long-term bonds—practically 20 times as much![2]

From the historical returns, stocks have a place in every portfolio. Looking back to the beginning of the 19th century indicates that stocks will beat returns of other investments by a healthy margin. If you have the nerve to stick with stocks even during the inevitable periodic downturns and you won't need the money for five or more years, you should consider putting that money into the stock market.

The percentage of your portfolio that you place into play with stocks is a measurable factor of your risk level. Even the most

---

[1]   Past performance is not a guarantee of future results.

[2]   S&P 500 Index

conservative investors need to have a small slice of their portfolio in the market to help counter inflation and interest risk. As we talked about in the last chapter, those two risks demand that your money needs to grow in order to keep up with the cost of living expenses. But to better determine your risk level; here is a sample questionnaire that we offer to our clients in helping them settle on a comfortable risk level.

The following is a typical questionnaire we offer our new clients in helping us determine their own personal risk level.

1. Your investment time horizon is an important consideration when constructing your investment strategy. How long will it be before you plan to use your investment for its intended purpose (i.e., college funding, retirement, etc.)?

   □ 0-2 years
   □ 3-5 years
   □ 6-0 years
   □ More than 10 years

2. Age is a very important determinant of portfolio selection. Please check your age.

   □ 35 or under (4)
   □ 36-45 (3)
   □ 46-55 (2)
   □ 56 or over (1)

3. How much of your current income comes from your investment portfolio?

   □ 0 (4)
   □ 1-24% (3)
   □ 25-50% (2)
   □ Over 50% (1)

4. How long could you cover your monthly living expenses with the cash and investments you currently have on hand?

- ☐ Less than 3 months (1)
- ☐ 3-12 months (2)
- ☐ 13-24 months (3)
- ☐ Over 2 years (4)

5. What is your and your spouse's/partner's annual income? (Total combined income before taxes.)

- ☐ Less than $25,000 (1)
- ☐ $25,000-$50,000 (2)
- ☐ $51,000-$100,000 (3)
- ☐ Over $100,000 (4)

6. What is the outlook for your earnings from sources other than investments over the next ten years?

- ☐ It will greatly decrease (1)
- ☐ It will decrease, but not by much (2)
- ☐ It will increase, but not by much (3)
- ☐ It will greatly increase (4)

7. Your investment objective summarizes the primary purpose of your investment. Which of the following best summarizes your overall investment philosophy?

- ☐ Take little or no risk (1)
- ☐ Achieve current income and growth with moderate risk (2)
- ☐ Achieve capital growth with some income and average risk (3)
- ☐ Achieve maximum capital growth with heightened risk (4)

8. Once you begin to make withdrawals from your portfolios, how long will the money in the account have to last?

    ☐ Less than 1 year (1)
    ☐ 1-5 years (2)
    ☐ 6-10 years (3)
    ☐ Over 10 years (4)

9. Please check the box that indicates your response to the following statement: "I am comfortable with investments that may go down in value from time to time, if they offer the potential for higher returns."

    ☐ Strongly disagree (1)
    ☐ Somewhat disagree (2)
    ☐ Somewhat agree (3)
    ☐ Strongly agree (4)

10. You are uncomfortable taking any risk with your investment.

    ☐ Strongly agree (1)
    ☐ Somewhat agree (2)
    ☐ Somewhat disagree (3)
    ☐ Strongly disagree (4)

11. Do you believe in buying and holding investments for the long-term (5 years or longer) regardless of how the markets change on a daily basis?

    ☐ Strongly disagree (1)
    ☐ Somewhat disagree (2)
    ☐ Somewhat agree (3)
    ☐ Strongly agree (4)

12. A month after you made an investment, its value decreases by 15%, would you:

   ☐ Sell it (1)
   ☐ Hold it until you break even, then sell it (2)
   ☐ Hold it (3)
   ☐ Hold it and buy more (4)

13. A month after you made an investment, its value increases by 25%, would you:

   ☐ Sell it and go to cash (1)
   ☐ Sell part and take some profits (2)
   ☐ Hold it (3)
   ☐ Hold it and buy more (4)

14. From your previous investment history, which of the following are you most comfortable with?

   ☐ Certificates of Deposit (1)
   ☐ Bonds (2)
   ☐ Bonds and stocks (3)
   ☐ Stocks (4)

15. Your intermediate and long-term goals are very important in determining your investment strategy. In the future do you think you'll need:

   ☐ No income from your investments (1)
   ☐ Less than your current income (2)
   ☐ The same as your current income (3)
   ☐ More than your current income (4)

Total Score = _____

Responses to the questionnaire provide an indication of your risk profile. The lowest that you can score is 14 and the highest is 56. Lower scores indicate a more risk adverse profile, while higher scores suggest the opposite. The range of possible scores has been divided into five groups, each of which reflects a different risk profile.

Total Score	Risk Profile
More than 50	Suggests an investor that is willing and able to assume risk and bear possible swings in share price. (100% Stocks)
41-50	Suggests willingness and ability to assume heightened risk in the form of equity exposure, spread across various equity asset classes. (80% Stocks / 20% Bonds)
29-40	Suggests moderate view towards investment risk. (60% Stocks / 40% Bonds)
21-28	Suggests willingness to take some risk, but still highly cautious. (40% Stocks / 60% Bonds)
20 or less	Suggests a highly risk adverse investor. Limited equity exposure and weighted toward fixed income. (20% Stocks / 80% Bonds)

📁 From The Real Life Files of Pat Vitucci

The following is a real life example where the names have been changed. But the situation described is accurate.

Robert is a 72 year old retiree enjoying his golden years in a beautiful retirement community. He plays golf twice a week, takes four vacations each year, and is the proud grandfather of three. As a widower, he lives alone, but is very involved with his two daughters and their family activities.

The date is March 15, 1997, and the mood in the country is similar to the roaring 20's: Happy days are here again! Many investors are getting enamored over the top story on the six o'clock news that frequently cites the stock pick of the day which doubled in value from just last month. This is an easy way to "get rich quick." Tired of not participating, Robert decides to buy just four of these "sure winners" that his stock broker offers with a modest amount of cash on hand. Just as the stock broker promised, Robert doubles his money practically overnight! Convinced there were special times and all the old rules of investing were passé, Robert was persuaded to invest the balance of his portfolio into more high tech opportunities. His portfolio grew to unprecedented levels and Robert was fully injected with "the irrational exuberance" bug, which many investors felt was genuine skill. We know how this story ends: Robert lost 80% of his portfolio's value by March 20, 2002.

Pat's Recommendation:

Robert may have forgotten that at the age of 72, diversification is extremely important. Diversification among asset classes, industry sectors, geography, income and growth and many other ways to slice up his portfolio, is essential to a good money management philosophy. Robert allowed his fear and greed, two emotions we struggle with on a daily basis, to completely guide his decisions. Your personal appetite for risk is the foundation parameter that a suitable portfolio is constructed with for any client.

Key Points from Chapter 2:

1. Before you invest, you need to determine how much risk you are comfortable with and then select investments that are based on that risk level.
2. You need to adjust your investments as needed to compliment your time frame.

3

Investment Product Knowledge

*It is better to have a permanent income than
to be fascinating.—Oscar Wilde*

In this chapter we'd like to offer a brief explanation about the typical investments offered today. You can use these products to fund your retirement account, put the kids through college, or simply as a means to building a reserve fund. Each of these products is suitable for different risk levels and some have additional risk factors as well.

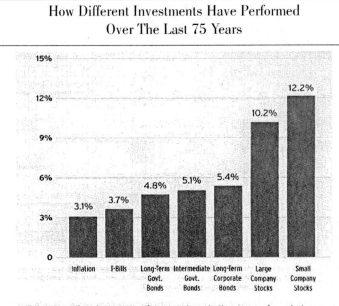

How Different Investments Have Performed
Over The Last 75 Years

While aggressive stocks outperform bonds and other types of asset classes, they are riskier than those in investments. Government bonds and Treasury bills are guaranteed by the U.S. Government if held to maturity.
Source: Ibbotson

Certificates of Deposit

A certificate of Deposit (CD) is a time deposit with a bank. Time deposits may not be withdrawn on demand like a check account. CDs are generally issued by commercial banks but they can be bought through brokerages. They bear a specific maturity date (from 3 months to 5 years), a specified interest rate, and can be issued in any denomination.

CDs offer a slightly higher yield than T-Bills because of the slightly higher default risk for a bank, but overall the likeliness of a large bank going broke is pretty slim. Of course, the amount of interest you earn depends on a number of factors such as the current interest rate environment, how much money you invest, the length of time, and your specific bank. While nearly every bank offers CDs, the rates are rarely competitive, so it's important to shop around.

The main advantage of CDs is their relative safety and knowing the return you'll receive. You'll generally earn more than in a savings account, and you won't be at the mercy of the stock market. Plus, in the U.S. the FDIC guarantees your investment up to $100,000. There are two main disadvantages to CDs. The returns are paltry and your money is tied up for the length of the CD. You can't get your money out without paying a harsh penalty.

Inflation-Protected CDs (CDIP)

A relatively new twist to CDs is the inflation-protected CDs. These are sold in $1,000 denominations and typically mature in five to ten years. As with regular CDs, CDIPs are federally insured up to $100,000. CDIPs pay a fixed interest rate. In addition, the principal is adjusted up or down for inflation, and the fixed interest is paid semiannually based on the adjusted principal. Investors owe taxes annually on the interest they receive and on the increase in the principal, despite the fact that principal increases aren't paid until maturity.

Bonds[7]

Bonds are known as "fixed-income" securities because the amount of income the bond will generate each year is "fixed" when the bond provides periodic payments or is sold. There are four basic kinds of bonds, all defined by who is the seller. The first bonds are sold by the U.S. government and their agencies. The second bonds are sold by corporations. Then there are bonds sold by state and local governments.

U.S. government bonds are called Treasuries because they are sold by the Treasury Department. Treasuries come in a variety

---

[7]   As interest rates rise, bond prices will fall. Any guarantee relates only to the prompt payment and interest and does not remove market risks if the investment is sold prior to maturity.

of different "maturities," or lengths of time until maturity, ranging from 3 months to 30 years. The various types are Treasury notes, Treasury bills, Treasury bonds, and inflation-indexed notes[8]. Each of these is based on maturity and amount of interest paid. The Treasury Department also sells savings bonds as well as other types of debt. Treasuries are guaranteed by the U.S. government and are free of state and local taxes on the interest they pay. Federal taxes are levied on these instruments.

Other government agencies, such as the Federal National Mortgage Association (Fannie Mae), the Federal Home Loan Mortgage Corporation (Freddie Mac), the Government National Mortgage Association (Ginnie Mae), and the Student Loan Association (Sallie Mae) sell bonds backed by the full faith and credit of the U.S. for specific purposes.

Companies sell debt through the public securities markets, the same as stocks. A company has quite a bit of flexibility as to how much debt it can issue and what interest it will pay. Corporate bonds normally carry higher interest rates than government bonds because there is the risk that the company could go bankrupt. High-yield bonds, also known as junk bonds, are corporate bonds issued by companies whose credit quality is below investment grade. Also, some companies offer convertible bonds—which can be converted into stock if certain provisions are met[9].

Because state and local governments can go bankrupt, they need to offer competitive rates just like corporate bonds. Unlike corporations, the only way a state can receive more income is to raise taxes. So the federal government permits states and local governments to sell bonds that are free of federal income tax on the interest paid. These municipal bonds can also have the state and local income taxes waived. What this means is that even though the municipal bonds may pay lower rates of interest, to a

---

[8]   U.S. Treasury bonds are backed by the full faith and credit of the U.S. Government if held to maturity.

[9]   As interest rates rise, bond prices will fall.

borrower in high tax brackets the bonds can actually have a higher after tax yield that other types of fixed income investments. These tax equivalent yields should be compared to other investments of similar risks[10].

Almost all investors who buy bonds buy them because they are generally safe investments. However, except for bonds from the federal government, bonds carry the potential risk of default, even though sometimes it can be quite remote. Bond ratings were developed as a way to indicate how financially stable the issuer of the bonds really is compared to its peer companies. Created by third parties like Standard and Poor's and Moody's, bond-rating services give bonds a letter or mixed letter and number rating based on the financial soundness of the bond issuer. We want to encourage you to always check the bonds' rating and be sure you're well versed in the rating system. The lower the rating on the bond will translate into a higher risk, which could affect the return on your "safe" investment.

Some examples:

AAA	Extremely strong capacity
AA	Very strong capacity
A	Strong capacity
BBB	Adequate capacity
BB	Ongoing uncertainty
B	Vulnerable to adverse conditions

Note: AAA, AA, A, & BBB are all considered "investment grade."

Stocks

Stocks are an easy way to own part of a company without ever having to show up for work or drive that long commute.

---

[10] Municipal bond income may be subject to Alternative Minimum Tax.

Shareholders own a part of the assets of the company and part of the money stream those assets generate. As with most things in life, the potential reward for owning stock in a growing business has some possible hazards. If the market goes bad, the company stock shares may decrease in value.

The New York Stock Exchange (NYSE) and the American Stock Exchange (AMEX) are both "listed" exchanges, meaning that the brokerage firms contribute individuals known as "specialists" who are responsible for all the trading in a specific stock. Volume, or the number of shares that trade on a given day, is counted by the specialist and reported to the exchange along with information on the price and size of each trade. The price is the highest amount any buyer is willing to pay at any given moment. When demand for a certain stock is high, the different buyers bid the price higher to induce sellers to sell. When demand for a stock is low, sellers must sell at lower prices to attract buyers and the price drops.

The over-the-counter market utilizes NASDAQ (National Association of Securities Dealers Automated Quotation) stock market and the OTC Bulletin Board by interacting over a centralized computer system managed by the NASDAQ. The difference in this market is that you are assured, except in extraordinary circumstances, you can always buy or sell your shares if the market is open. The system matches buyers and sellers electronically and the transfer of ownership is completed.

Common Stock versus Preferred Stock

Common stock is a security that represents ownership in a company. The holders of common stock exercise control by being able to elect the board of directors and voting on corporate policy. Preferred stock is also an equity security that represents ownership in a company. One of the differences is that preferred stock is issued with a stated dividend, which must be paid prior to dividends that are paid to common stockholders. Preferred stock does not carry any voting rights. Most of the individual stocks that investors purchase are common stocks. Preferred stocks are often used by companies in benefit packages for senior employees and officers.

The most common way to buy individual stocks is through a brokerage account. Again, this is an easy way for you to become a partial owner of a company. But, is that a risk you want to assume in buying a company that you may not understand its product line, management philosophy, or any other important criteria for selecting and owning that stock?

Mutual Funds

A mutual fund is simply a collection of stocks and/or bonds. Most mutual funds have a fund manager who is charged with the task of adhering to the fund's defined objective and makes trades in order to maintain that directive. If you invest in a mutual fund you will pay a fee to the fund manager each year to complete these transactions.

Several times a year you can see on popular financial advice magazines headlines which read: "The Top 20 Mutual Funds of the Year," or "The Only 12 Mutual Funds You'll Ever Need," or another favorite, "The 5 Best Mutual Funds." Amazingly, it is rare that any of these articles will ever mention the same funds. The warning phrase "let the buyer beware" is never truer than with investments. So be careful that the mutual funds' objective is in align with your goals and investment plans.

Mutual funds do offer a great investment advantage: diversification[11]. When you buy an individual company stock you essentially have all your eggs in one basket. But with a mutual fund, you have spread your money out over a variety of companies and industries. Mutual funds are available in every possible combination you can imagine. But they can be defined into five basic categories.

- Bond mutual funds are pooled amounts of money invested in bonds.
- Balanced mutual funds have a mixture of stocks and bonds.

---

[11]   Diversification does not ensure against loss.

- General mutual funds are typically labeled by the size of the companies they invest in: small, mid, or large.
- International mutual funds invest in companies that are based outside of the U.S.
- Sector mutual funds invest in one particular business sector; such as health care, technology, Latin American Fund, growth or income funds.

Open-End Mutual Funds versus Closed-End Investment Companies

Both open-ended and closed-ended funds sell shares to the public, the difference between them hinges on the type of securities that they market, and where investors buy and sell their shares in the primary or secondary markets.

The following chart highlights the some of the differences:

	Open-End	Closed-End
Capitalization	Unlimited, continuous offering of shares	Fixed, single offering of shares
Issues	Common stock only	Common stock, preferred stock, or debt securities
Shares	Full or fractional	Full only
Offerings & Trading	Sold & redeemed by fund only. Continuous primary offering	Initial primary offering. Secondary trading OTC or on an exchange
Pricing	Selling price determined as set in the prospectus	Price determined by supply & demand
Shareholder Rights	Dividends (when declared), voting	Dividends (when declared), voting, preemptive

Unit Investment Trusts (UIT)

A unit investment trust is an investment company organized under a trust indenture and identified by several characteristics. UITs do not have boards of directors, employ investment advisors, or actively manage their portfolios. A UIT functions as a holding company for its investors. Each share is an undivided interest in the entire underlying portfolio. Because UITs are not managed, when any securities in the portfolio are liquidated, the proceeds must be distributed.

There are also index mutual funds which seek to match the market by buying representative amounts of each stock in the index. For example, an S&P 500 Index Fund would invest in securities to mirror the S&P 500. An index fund buys and sells securities in a manner that mirrors the composition of the selected index. The fund's performance tracks the underlying index's performance. Turnover of securities in an index fund's portfolio is minimal. As a result, an index fund generally has lower management costs than other types of funds. Be aware, however, if you're considering investing in a mutual fund to be sure to compare its expense ratio against other similar funds.

Mutual funds charge fees. The mutual fund's expense ratio is the most important fee to understand. It is composed of the following:

- The management fee is the money used to pay the managers of the mutual fund.
- Administrative costs are the costs of recordkeeping, mailing, maintaining the customer service line, etc.
- The 12b-1 distribution fee which pays for marketing, advertising, and distribution fees.

When you are purchasing a mutual fund be sure to look at these fee components, this will give you a ratio to compare funds. For actively managed funds the number will be higher than for most index funds. In addition, there are load (cost to purchase) and no-load (no cost to purchase) mutual funds available. All of these small percentages can quickly add up, so be sure you are clear about a mutual fund's true cost before you add it to your portfolio.

Annuities

Annuities are generally suitable for more long-term investing. These investments are typically available in three-, five-, and seven-year increments. One of the greatest advantages of annuities is tax deferral. Fixed annuities earn a fixed rate of interest for a defined length of time that is not taxed until withdrawn[12].

Variable annuities are similar to fixed annuities in that current premiums may be traded for a future stream of income. However, instead of earning fixed rates of interest, the growth of a variable annuity is based on the performance of investment sub-accounts that you select. A variable annuity can have additional features that will provide you with protection and help your beneficiaries.

- Principal guarantee—allows your heirs to inherit the amount of money you initially deposited into the account.
- Maximum anniversary value—each year the annuity takes the "high water mark" value and insures that value as the amount your heirs will inherit.

Again, a variable annuity is ideal for the long-term investor. There can be penalties if you try to withdraw your money prior to the agreed time frame. But the many advantages offered versus a plain mutual fund can make this a very attractive investment for many people[13].

Retirement Plans

Individual Retirement Accounts (IRA) is one of a group of plans that allow you to put some of your income into a tax-deferred retirement fund—meaning you won't pay taxes until you withdraw the money.

Roth IRA is a new type of retirement account that differs from the conventional IRA in that it provides no tax deduction up front on the contributions. Instead, it offers total exemption

---

[12] Withdrawals of tax-deferred accumulations are subject to ordinary income tax, and a 10% penalty may apply for withdrawals before age 59 ½.

[13] Guarantee is based on the claims-paying ability of the insurer.

from federal and state taxes when you cash out to pay for retirement or a first home.

401(k) and the 403(b) are common retirement vehicles offered by employers. Each is named after the Internal Revenue Code section in which it is covered. This should be one of the first investments on your list if you are eligible. Many companies also encourage their employees by offering a company match program. Be sure to take advantage of these offers, it is one of the few times in life you'll be able to get "free money."

The Keogh is a special type of IRA that doubles as a pension plan for the self-employed. This allows the self-employed to put aside much more than the limited amounts allowed for an IRA.

The Solo 401(k) is a new way to allow certain self-employed individuals to contribute significantly more to their retirement savings. An estimated 17.6 million Americans are eligible to participate in this new retirement plan. This includes incorporated and unincorporated businesses, such as sole proprietors, partnerships, and corporations. Examples include consultants, lawyers, accountants, doctors, electricians, and real estate agents. The Solo, or Individual, 401(k) offers many benefits:

- Employer/owner may contribute up to $40,000 per year, depending on their income.
- As with traditional 401(k) plans, contributions are made with pretax dollars and contributions and earnings grow tax-deferred until withdrawn.
- Employer/owners can make salary deferrals equal to 100% of compensation, up to a maximum of $11,000. The maximum will increase by $1,000 per year until 2006, when the maximum reaches $15,000.
- Employer/owners may also make company profit-sharing contributions of up to 25% of their salary.
- Employer/owners who are age 50 and over may contribute an additional "catch-up" contribution of $1,000 annually. This can be in addition to the $40,000 maximum. The

catch-up contribution maximum will increase by $1,000 per year until 2006, when the maximum reaches $5,000.

Finally, the Simplified Employee Pension (SEP) Plan is a unique type of Keogh retirement plan. SEPs were created so that the small business owner could set up a retirement plan that would be easier to administer than a normal pension plan. Both employees and the employer can contribute to a SEP.

Real Estate Investment Trusts (REIT)

There are two basic categories of REITs: equity REITs and mortgage REITs. An equity REIT is a publicly traded company that, as its principal business, buys, manages, renovates, maintains, and occasionally sells real properties. It also acquires properties and frequently develops new properties when the economics are favorable. It is tax advantaged in that it is not taxed on the corporate level, and, by law, must pay out at least 90% of its net income as dividends to its investors. A mortgage REIT is a REIT that makes and holds loans and other obligations that are secured by real estate collateral.

It is important to not only be aware of the many types of investment products available, but also to be sure you are utilizing the best product for reaching your goal. Some of the above mentioned products have penalties attached if you withdraw your money prior to the end of the contract, or before reaching age 59 ½. Again, we tried to provide you with an overview of some of the most common investment products available. We want to encourage you to talk over your choices with a knowledgeable financial advisor prior to any investing.

Lifecycle Funds

For the investor that is overwhelmed with all of these choices and is looking for a combination of stocks and bonds in one product, the new lifecycle funds could offer a unique opportunity.

Some have target retirement dates, and their stock-bond mix becomes increasingly conservative as that date approaches. It's up to the investor to pick the fund that makes the most sense, given their time horizon and tolerance for risk. Again, we want to warn you DON'T INVEST AND FORGET. Even with these, you'll want to do your homework. Lifecycle funds were intended primarily for participants in 401(k) and similar employer-sponsored retirement plans. But if you plan to purchase one of these funds outside of a 401(k) and you are in a high tax bracket, you probably want to keep the fund in your individual retirement account. Why? Lifecycle funds invest their bond position in taxable bonds. That can translate into an unnecessary large tax bite for some investors, especially the folks in the 33% or 35% federal income tax brackets. These funds can offer you a core for your portfolio and help you keep on target with your time horizon.

Key Points from Chapter 3:

1. There are many different investment products to choose from that will easily allow you to reach your financial goals.
2. By diversifying your investment choices you can take advantage of the market changes in several sectors.
3. Be sure to take advantage of tax deferred investments.

4

Debt

*I'm living so far beyond my income that we may almost be said
to be living apart.—e.e. cummings*

To most folks debt can be a huge shackle. However, it shouldn't be that way. If you have found yourself in debt, for what ever reason, you fully understand the weight it carries. We will not lecture you about how you need to be vigilant in your savings and how debt can inhibit your ability to get ahead financially. We know you've heard all of those speeches before. We do want to clarify the difference between "good" and "bad" debt.

First the bad news: Bad debt can be simply defined as any debt you are paying interest on that depreciates in value and is not tax deductible. Typical examples are buying a car on time and credit cards. As you're aware, the minute you drive that shiny, new set of wheels off the dealer's lot—it has dropped in value by as much as 20%. Each time that you don't pay off your credit card in full, you're paying interest—interest that is going into the pockets of the credit card company, not yours.

Why do most folks borrow money? Simple, because they don't have enough money to buy something they want or need. What we want you to be aware of is the difference between borrowing for something that represents a long-term investment and borrowing for consumption. If you spend, $1500 on a vacation, the money is gone by the time your flight lands back home. Poof! We hope you have some wonderful Kodak moments to remember, but you'll not have any financial value to show for it. Now, we're not saying don't take vacations. In fact, we want you to enjoy life and as a popular airline advertisement touts, "feel free to travel about the country." But, if you had to borrow money in the form of an outstanding balance on your credit card for many months, then you could not afford the vacation you took.

We refer to debt incurred for consumption as bad debt. Don't get us wrong—you're not a bad person for having debt, but the debt is harmful to your long-term financial health. You'll be able to take many more vacations during your lifetime if you save the cash in advance to afford them. If you get in the habit of borrowing and paying all that interest for vacations, cars, clothing, and other consumer items, you'll spend more of your future income paying back the debt and interest. So you'll have less money available for vacations and all your other goals.

When was the last time you heard someone say that he decided to forego a purchase because he was saving toward retirement or a home purchase? Doesn't happen often, does it?

So hopefully you realize the possible ramifications of "bad" debt. But we also want to remind you of how it can also affect your future. With bad debt, you are also inhibiting your money from being able to work for you. Since each month you are using your money to pay off bad debt, you are not able to use that money to invest for your future and allow it to grow.

Now that we've discussed how "bad" debt can hinder you, we'd like to talk about how "good" debt can help you reach your goals. Again, let's define what "good" debt is: any debt that you are paying for that provides an increase in value. Typical examples of this kind of debt would be a mortgage or college loan. With a mortgage, you are paying on an asset that will most likely increase in value and may be tax deductible, thereby lowering the net cost of that loan. Naturally, your home is more to you than an asset on a balance sheet. And with a college loan, it is an investment in your future and earnings potential. Both of these examples are not liquid assets that you can readily see a quick profit from, but they each offer you a way to grow your net worth for the future.

Here are a few thoughts to consider regarding why not to pay off your mortgage:

- Paying off your mortgage faster has no tax benefit. However, putting additional money into a tax-deductible retirement plan can immediately reduce your federal and state income taxes.
- In order for you to have a reasonable chance of earning more on your investments than it's costing you to borrow on a mortgage, you must be aggressive with your investments.
- Typically, paying down your mortgage depletes your emergency reserves. Paying an extra $100 per month on your mortgage may appear to be a prudent course of action, but actually, economically, it is not recommended. (You should be commended for your discipline; simply re-direct that discipline to an investment that will appreciate and is liquid.)
- Real estate appreciation actually lowers the real cost of your loan.
- Finally, don't be hood-winked by thinking that somehow you'll be protected by a real estate crash if you pay down your mortgage sooner. If real estate prices collapse, you suffer the full effect of a price decline, regardless of your mortgage size.

We'd like to mention a relatively new tool, especially for those folks who have celebrated their 62nd birthday: reverse mortgages. Rising home values and low returns on income investments have increased the number of older homeowners seeking reverse mortgages as a way to tap into the equity in their homes. There are several restrictions and a variety of loan options, namely a lump sum, a credit line, a monthly advance or a combination of the three. There are maximums on the amounts of these loans and an additional set of obligations in contrast to a "regular" mortgage. But, we wanted to alert our readers that this option is out there and might be just the ticket for your situation. Of course, good sources to contact for further information is your local AARP office or a mortgage broker who specializes in this type of loan.

Yes, we know how often you are probably bombarded with the lures and enticements to increase your debt. But just for a few minutes we'd like to offer you an encouraging word about the power and beauty of eliminating debt, namely the "bad" debt. Consumer debt is hazardous to reaching your long-term financial goals because it allows you to borrow against your future earnings. Borrowing via credit cards, auto loans, and the like are also one of the most expensive ways to borrow money.

Having met and counseled clients in making investment decisions, many with modest economic means, a few common themes have developed. We'd like to share the characteristics that these people who have built wealth have demonstrated:

- Living within their means and systematically saving and investing money, typically in tax-favorable products.
- Buying and holding stocks, ideally through mutual funds.
- Building their own small business or career
- Investing in real estate

That kind of common sense investing is a great endorsement for the division between good and bad debt. It's always a great lesson when we can learn from others. These clients have not only shown that the four characteristics listed above are possible, regardless of how the media might profess otherwise, but that the common sense shown will be instrumental in building wealth for a secure retirement.

We've also met plenty of high-income earners, even some who take home a six or seven-figure paychecks annually, who have very little to invest. So, the difference in those that invest isn't based on their income. It's simply based on their ability to save a portion of what they've earned. If you're not a high-income earner, it's tempting to think that you can't save. Even if you are blessed with a high income, you may think that you'll be better able to save more if you can bump up your income. Although this may be true, this way of thinking is a crutch. Remember the days before you earned your current big paycheck. Did you have enough at the end of each month then? Did you think the key to financial nirvana would be a raise at work? Well, if you did get the raise and you're still scrambling at the end of the month to pay Peter and Paul, perhaps you need to re-evaluate your budgeting skills. Again, think about what you are paying each month on "bad" debt versus what you are paying each month on "good" debt.

Here's another tidbit for you to consider: Most lenders are overly concerned with your debt load. A lot of debt, such as credit cards or auto loans not only diminishes your funds, but also their outlook on viewing you favorably for future loans. Lenders know that having "bad" debt increases the possibility that you may fall behind or actually default on your loan payments.

Consumer debt is bad news even without considering that it hurts your financial records. It is at a high cost and it encourages you to live beyond your means. Unlike the interest on mortgage debt, consumer debt interest is not tax deductible. Rein in your spending and adjust to living within your means.

Jean Chatzky, in her book "*You Don't Have to Be Rich*," points out, "The difference between spenders and savers lies not so much in their demographic makeup, but in their habits and knowledge. Savers are more likely than spenders to be happy with their lifestyle, self esteem, even their appearance. They're more likely to feel confident and content, less likely to feel stressed and restless." (p. 129) The fact remains: You can only save if you're living within your means. Most people don't. Hopefully, we've convinced you to become financially fit. Ms. Chatzky outlines "The 10 Commandments of Financial Happiness" in her book. (p. 226)

1. Get (pretty) organized. You just have to come up with a system that you understand.
2. Pay bills as they come in, rather than all at once.
3. Keep tabs on your cash, so you'll know where your money is going.
4. Save at least 5% of your household income.
5. Protect your family (and yourself.) Doing all you can to shelter yourself from financial hardship in the future is also an important part of financial happiness.
6. Rid your life of revolving credit card debt.
7. Do unto others—by volunteering, giving away money or donating old belongings—can add to your own happiness.
8. Spend sensibly. Spending no more than you can afford is crucial for financial happiness.
9. Start working toward your goals now!
10. Communicate with your partner can help you (and them) move towards a more peaceful existence and future.

Saving money is really only half the battle. The other half is making your money grow. Over long time periods, earning just a few percent more makes a big difference in the size of your nest egg. Earning inflation-beating returns is easy to do if you're willing to invest in stocks, real estate, and small businesses. Ownership investments (stocks, real estate, and small businesses) have historically generated returns greater than the inflation rate by 6% or more, while lending investments (savings accounts and bonds) tend to be at or frequently below inflation.

Recently a note-worthy book, *"The Two-Income Trap: Why Middle-Class Mothers & Fathers are Going Broke"* was written by the mother-daughter team of Elizabeth Warren and Amelia Warren Tyagi. In there book, the authors point out some startling statistics (p. 179):

- The average middle-class family can no longer buy a house without putting both husband and wife to work.
- Parents with young children are more than twice as likely to go bankrupt than any other segment of the population.
- More than 90% of those families in bankruptcy would qualify as middle-class.

The author's research indicates that long before a financial disaster strikes—job loss, illness or divorce—the families were already vulnerable. "They are financially fragile because so much of their two incomes are devoted to mortgages for homes bought in a shrinking number of desirable school districts. The rest of their money is being used to cover health insurance and preschool and college tuitions, and to pay the loan on a second car." The authors proceed to advise anyone in this situation to hold a "financial fire drill." And they offer these three key questions:

1. Can you survive without one income for six months?
2. Can you cut fixed expenses?
3. Do you have a backup plan?

The authors are not out to scare families, but rather want to provide a wake-up call on what steps are needed for consideration before facing financial disaster at home.

🗁 From The Real Life Files of Pat Vitucci
The following is a real life example where the names have been
changed. But the situation described is accurate.

Peter and Marion are 62 years old. They are a happily married couple, living in a wonderful suburb. For many years, they have paid extra money on their monthly mortgage payment. Their savings account only represents approximately two months of monthly reserve. Their children are grown and are on their own now. Unfortunately, Peter, who is the major breadwinner in the family, was recently downsized from his high-paying engineering job. His prospects for finding a similar position are fairly unattractive given the state of his industry, with many jobs being exported to foreign markets. Additionally, Peter will suffer from age bias when interviewing for a new position. While Peter and Marion should be congratulated on their disciplined savings plan, unfortunately it was not directed properly. When Peter lost his job, the bank holding the mortgage continued to expect to receive the monthly mortgage payment, despite all of those extra dollars sent in previous years. Their reserve was not adequate to continue paying the mortgage each month. Refinancing was also difficult, if not impossible, option given their new much lower income.

Pat's Recommendation:

Regularity of investing is admirable. We encourage folks to direct extra monthly dollars into a collection of mutual funds, which have historically grown at a rate of 11% annually. This will be their reserve for emergencies or an additional source to withdraw in retirement.

Importantly, the 6% mortgage from their bank actually has a net asset after deductibility on their IRS 1040 form of only 4.25%. After netting out the real estate appreciation of 4.25% annually, the real cost of that 6% mortgage after IRS deductibility and real estate appreciation is ZERO! *Why would anyone pay someone a loan back early when they are borrowing at zero cost?*

Key Points from Chapter 4:

1. The cost of a debt is not only monetarily, but also mentally by preventing peace of mind.
2. Large debts can prevent you from being able to enjoy a comfortable retirement, since you are spending the money today versus saving it for tomorrow.
3. Be sure that the debts you have are "good" debts and will not restrict your retirement livelihood.

5

Components of a Financial Plan

Lack of money is no obstacle.
Lack of an idea is an obstacle.—Ken Hakuta

When you make investment decisions, you always face uncertainty. Will the economy grow at a healthy pace or slow to a crawl? Will stocks surge to new highs or stumble? No matter what happens, your life goes on. There's still a child's education to finance, a mortgage to pay and a retirement nest egg to accumulate. Creating a financial plan is the most vital first step every investor can take. But with the multitude of investment choices, "what's an investor to do?" Everyone wants to take advantage of market gains, and minimize their exposure to market losses.

First, remember that shifts in economic growth and fluctuations in the financial markets are normal parts of the U.S. economy's business cycle. They've happened before and they will happen again. While one-time events—such as a sudden move in the markets—usually receive extensive media coverage, long-term success stories rarely receive the same attention.

The Stock Market Spin Cycles

The stock market has created what some market analysts claim are patterns and cycles that they use to predict market trends. Naturally these claims gather media attention from time to time. For example, there are some to tout that during the third year of a presidential term the market will be strong and show noticeable gains. Then there are those who believe in seasonal cycles, advocating "buy in October and sell in May."

The realization is that stocks move based on business fundamentals. Granted, there can be increased exuberance from time to time based on: the political issues, economic issues, emotional feelings, and an entire spectrum of the other issues that affect Wall Street. It remains that people are continually looking for a crystal ball to predict financial security. Reliance on these cycles is not good investing analysis because you are ignoring the basic economic and business fundamentals that should be the foundation for your investment choices and portfolio building.

Successful investors develop a well-reasoned, long-range investment plan and stick to it. While a financial plan won't make you wealthy overnight, it can help you reach your investment goals over time. The following are some basic ideas for you to start implementing your plan.

1. Define your investment objectives. Begin by asking yourself these two questions: What is my investment horizon? What do I want from my investment?
2. Know your tolerance for investment risk. When choosing investments, remember one thing: The greater the risk, the greater the potential for reward. Are you comfortable

risking some of your principal for a potentially greater reward? Or would you prefer a lower return in exchange for greater safety of principal? In general, the longer your investment horizon, the greater the risk you can tolerate. Your financial advisor can also help you understand the risks of various types of investments.

3. Build a portfolio that fits your objectives and risk tolerance. No one mix of investments is ideal for everyone. You should construct a portfolio tailored to your particular financial needs and risk tolerance. Be sure your program is flexible enough so that it can be modified as your investment needs change over time. Keep in mind that your investment professional can help you create an investment program that suits your financial situation and objectives.

An important aspect of any financial plan is to take a full overview of your entire financial life. Don't make the mistake of just looking at your 401(k) and say "that's it!" Be sure you review your monthly budget items along with your long-range goals in creating a true picture for your financial plan. In addition, start to map out what pieces of your puzzle you wish to add and how those investments will be funded.

Few people enjoy creating a budget, yet it is sometimes those same people that face retirement without enough money. A good place to start is by determining what percentage of your money you are saving. Whether it is high, low, or (hopefully not) negative, you'll have a starting point. Now you can begin to see what your choices are: perhaps you will choose to spend less; or you will decide to somehow earn more. Whatever path you choose today will begin to set your course for the tomorrows to come.

Also, be sure to take advantage of all the easy ways you can save money that you can. For example, maximize your 401(k) contributions at work. One of the beautiful benefits of this is that the money is deducted from your paycheck before you even see it (or have the chance to spend it.) Generally you can also do this with your bank to build up your emergency savings account. Have a certain percentage or dollar amount placed into your savings account each month. Finally, one of most people's most overlooked ways to save for retirement and develop a financial plan is to eliminate credit card debt from their life. The interest you are paying on the credit card balance is money that should be working for you—not against you.

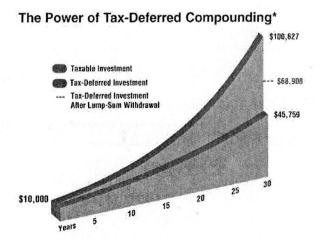

*Assumes 8% return

If you enjoy spending money and living for today, we hope you will be motivated to start saving today. The longer you wait to save, the more you will ultimately need to save.

The benefits of working with a financial advisor are many. But the primary ones are all relate to working with an educated, trained professional that can provide you with informed, objective advice. The financial advisor you choose should also engage you in an active relationship that offers ongoing service for every aspect of your financial life. Since you are entrusting this person in a dialogue for making your investment decisions, be sure that they are someone you wish to work with for the long term.

Some additional tips when interviewing a financial advisor:

1. Ask about their investment philosophy, to determine how it aligns with your thinking.

2. Ask to talk to a couple of their clients.
3. Explain what you are seeking in a financial advisor.
4. Make sure that they have a personality that is compatible with yours.

Remember, this is someone you want to work with on a long-term relationship. Feel free to take your time and be sure of your decision, rather than regret it later.

Knowing how to analyze and select investments is only half the battle. How much of each should be in your portfolio? Complicated, contradictory, and confusing asset allocation models abound in the investment world. Many times these models appear to be designed by a committee of dueling economists who have agreed upon adding a small dash of every investment option imaginable rather than to give investors guidance in how to divvy up their investment pie. So, what is the average-guy investor to do?

The key to all asset allocation models is risk. Remember that risk is a measurement of how willing you are to see the value of your investments decrease in the near term, even while you know the chances that they will increase over the long term. The higher the risk in an investment, the more likely it is to drop in the short term as well as rise.

In modern finance, risk is defined as the variability of returns. If an asset jumps up and down a lot, it is deemed to be riskier than an asset that stays put or climbs slowly—even if the asset that jumps around a lot tends to outperform the slower moving assets over time. When your returns are more variable, you have more of a chance of losing money.

Stocks, by and large, have outperformed everything else over long periods of time. When investing more than 10 or 20 years in stocks, you are almost certain to outperform anything else. Investors who use asset allocation models that are concerned about short-term volatility under-perform over the long term because these models will inevitably take them out of stocks and put them into other investments like bonds.

So, what's the deal if you can lose money on securities over short periods of time, why invest in them all? Why not stick to safe investments and let it lie? Well, once again let us refer to our favorite history lesson. Long-term historical returns that investment vehicles like stocks have generated (hopefully) have swayed you to sticking with them.

The difference in annual returns between stocks and bonds is magnified over long periods of time. Because of the miracle of compounding, each year you are left with slightly more money that is then reinvested at a higher rate of return, and that extra money earns more money. Over the period from 1950 to 1995, an investor would have earned a total return of 19,300% in stocks versus 523% in long-term bonds[1]. That's almost 20 times as much!

As you can discern from the historical returns listed above, stocks have a place in every portfolio. The historical record stretching back to the beginning of the 19th century indicates that stocks will beat returns of other investment by a healthy margin. If you have the intestinal fortitude to stick with stocks even during the inevitable periodic downturns and you have money that you will not need for five years or more, you should consider putting that money in a diversified portfolio. Some of the typical components we utilize are:

Stocks
     Large Cap
     Mid Cap
     Small Cap
     International
Bonds
     Short Term
     Long Term
Utilities
Real Estate (such as REITs)
Cash (such as money markets)

---

[1]   S&P 500.

It is the individual percentages of each component that will make your portfolio unique. Determining your percentages is tied to several things: such as your risk level, your age, your goals, and your time horizon. Foolishly many people think that once those percentages have been determined "that's it—I'm done." But wait—there's more! DON'T INVEST AND FORGET. One of the main principles in the asset allocation model is to monitor and review your portfolio. Just as these percentages and allocations are the right fit for you today, they might become uncomfortable in a few years. We know that you have the oil changed in your car every 3,000 miles, visit the dentist every six months, and eagerly schedule your annual exam with your physician each and every year. So it should not come as a surprise that as your body and life changes and evolves—so too do your investments. For example, Utilities might be a great place to have say 15% of your investment pie this year. So you leave it there for years. Good luck! We'll say it again—DON'T INVEST AND FORGET. Reviewing your portfolio needs to be conducted with regularity throughout the year. Go ahead and mark your calendar now for at least a monthly review of your allocations.

Finally, we'd like to leave you with some suggestions of common dangers to avoid:

1. Do nothing. There is no guarantee that the market will go up when you invest. But we can guarantee you one thing: doing nothing at all will not provide you with the retirement of your dreams.
2. Not starting now. Postponing your investing career is second only to doing nothing. The earlier you start the better off you'll be.
3. Investing before paying down credit card debt. Since many of these cards have an annual interest rate of 16-21%. If you have $5000 to invest, but you also have a $5000 credit card debt. Pay off the debt, then invest.
4. Investing for the short term. Invest money in the stock market that you won't need for at least three years, and

preferably five years or longer. If you'll need your cash next year or sooner, use a money market account or CD to keep your money safe until then.

5. Turning down free money. You'd never turn down a dollar if someone offered it to you with no strings attached. Yet, that's exactly what you're doing if your company offers a 401(k) or similar retirement savings plan with an employer match and you're not participating. Always participate in any tax-advantaged, employer-matched savings programs.

6. Playing it safe. If you're young, most of your investing dollars should be in the stock market. You have enough time to weather any dips in the market and to reap the rewards of long-term gains. Although you may want to transition a portion of your portfolio into bonds later in life as you depend on your investments for income, stocks should make up a large portion of the portfolio of every investor.

7. Playing it scary. Not every investment is for everyone. Even if you're a somewhat of a daredevil, you shouldn't pour all of your money into something that could end up going down the drain.

8. Viewing collectibles or lottery tickets as investments. If old comic books, Barbie dolls, and abandoned exercise equipment could be used to fund retirements, do you think the stock market would have existed this long? Probably not. Don't make the mistake of thinking that your jewelry, cherished childhood toys, or the lottery will provide you with a comfortable retirement in your later years.

9. Trading in and out of the market. We believe the best approach to investing is the long-term. Pick your investments well and you'll be able to reap the rewards over the years. Trade in and out of the market and you'll be saddled with fees that chip away at your returns, and you'll probably miss out on gains that long-term investors will be enjoying with far fewer hassles and losses. Re-allocation decisions within the market are essential, but moving all of your money into cash is not

recommended. Trying to time the market for cash to equity or fixed income positions, statistically, has not worked well for the last 75 years. Tomorrow is probably not going to be very different.

As Harry Dent wrote in his book, *The Roaring 2000s*, "Money or economic wealth is ultimately about giving yourself the freedom to choose the lifestyle that you want and to champion the causes you believe in. That is the new ethic in this era of prosperity when many of us have already achieved the fundamentals of survivals, security, and living. The ability to greatly evolve and advance one's standard of living has not always been possible for many people throughout history. We are living in the greatest period of change and progress since the printing press revolution and the discovery of America and the rest of the world after the late 1400s. Such times create the greatest opportunity for advancement of people from all socioeconomic sectors. The greatest advances in such times have often come from the drive and motivation of lower-class people and penniless immigrants. 80% of the millionaires today were self-made through either systematic investment from above average, not extreme, incomes or from entrepreneurial business." (p. 22)

🗁 From The Real Life Files of Pat Vitucci
The following is a real life example where the names have been changed. But the situation described is accurate.

Anthony and Elizabeth are 48 and 46 years old, respectively, and have been married for 23 years. Their two sons are both in college; ages 19 and 21. Anthony is the Vice President of his firm and earns $625,000 per year, contributes the maximum to his 401(k), currently holds a $2 million Universal Life insurance policy and routinely saves $1500 per month via an electronic sweep of his checking account into his investment account.

Elizabeth is a high school biology teacher, who absolutely loves her job, earns $45,000 per year and contributes the maximum to her 403b Tax Deferred Plan.

Anthony and Elizabeth own their current home, valued at approximately $750,000 and have a mortgage balance of $234,000. Their vacation home is in the mountains and its' current market value is $180,000 with a mortgage balance of $77,000. They have funded their sons' college tuition with student loans and partially offset by UGMA custodial accounts that they are now taking systematic withdrawals from to pay for books, tuition and fees.

Both Anthony's and Elizabeth's parents live nearby in a retirement village, are in their early 80s, and enjoy reasonably good health. Occasionally, they need to intervene in their parents' lives and assist with financial or medical issues as they arise.

It is very evident that Anthony and Elizabeth have very busy lives juggling professional careers, parenting, maintaining two homes, looking after parents, and trying to enjoy some relaxation time. Unfortunately, while they continue to be good stewards of their money by saving regularly, they have not made decisions to re-deploy their assets based on the direction of the market. At the end of the day, they don't have the time, passion, or energy to read the Wall Street Journal, Barrons, Fortune, and other financial sources to ascertain whether to move their holdings based on the direction of the market.

Pat's Recommendation:

Despite Anthony and Elizabeth's excellent financial records, they have neglected to carefully manage their assets. Neither Anthony nor Elizabeth have reviewed their company 401(k) and 403b, respectively, to determine if their payroll deductions are being properly directed into stocks, bonds, etc, positions. Additionally, Anthony's monthly $1500 has been misguided for at least the last 24 months, given the change in the market direction. The couple should hire a fee-based advisor that is independent, non-salaried by any company and has a personality that is compatible with theirs. Reviews with the advisor should be scheduled regularly and compared their performance with the industry benchmarks.

Key Points from Chapter 5:

1. Take the time to develop a plan for your long range goals in order that you can realistically reach them.
2. Put the power of tax deferral and compound interest to work on your side.
3. Regularly revisit your financial plan to determine if you are still "on target" or if adjustments are needed.

6

Tax Efficiency for Your Plan

Money is better than poverty, if only for financial reasons.
—*Woody Allen*

Tax efficiency is being able to keep more of what you earn. Taxes can take a big bite out of investment returns. One way to shield your investment income from taxes is by investing in municipal bonds. Income on most municipal bonds is tax free at the federal level, and in many cases, can offer state and local tax relief as well (may sometimes be subject to the alternative minimum tax). A financial advisor can help you tailor your portfolio to meet your financial objectives, time horizon and risk tolerance. In this chapter we'd like to explore some of the avenues you can utilize for tax efficiency.

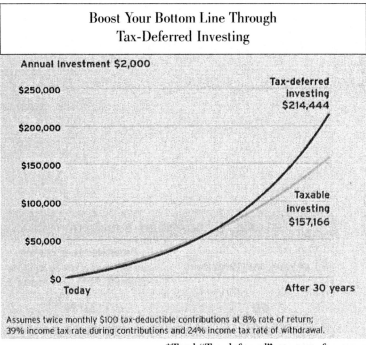

**Boost Your Bottom Line Through
Tax-Deferred Investing**

Annual Investment $2,000

Tax-deferred
investing
$214,444

$250,000

$200,000

$150,000

Taxable
investing
$157,166

$100,000

$50,000

$0
Today   After 30 years

Assumes twice monthly $100 tax-deductible contributions at 8% rate of return;
39% income tax rate during contributions and 24% income tax rate of withdrawal.

*Total "Tax deferred" amount after taxes

Tax-deferral means earnings are not taxed until they are actually withdrawn. As a result, your investment will accumulate faster than a similar taxable investment because it will avoid the erosive effects of current taxation on interest, dividends, and capital gains. By postponing taxes until after your peak earning years, you could be taxed at a lesser rate, as your tax bracket is likely to be lower in your retirement years.

Taking advantage of saving and investing in tax-deductible retirement accounts should be your number one personal financial priority (unless you're still paying off high-interest credit cards). Once money is in a retirement account, any interest, dividends, and appreciation grow inside the account without being taxed. You defer taxes on all the accumulating gains and profits until you withdraw the money down the road, which you can do without penalty after age 59 ½. In the meantime, the more money you have working for you, rather than that money being paid to the government.

One of the biggest mistakes that people at all income levels make with retirement accounts is not taking advantage of them at a younger age. The sooner you start to save, the less painful it is each year to save enough to reach your goals because your contributions have more years to compound and grow. Each decade you delay approximately doubles the percentage of your earnings you should save to meet your goals.

Example:

If you start by saving 5% per year in your twenties, compounding will allow you to reach your retirement goal, but waiting until your thirties may mean socking away 10% per year. And then by postponing until your forties you may need to save 20% each year. Instead, let compound interest work for you!

In general, the higher your tax bracket, the more you may benefit from tax-free income earned on municipal bonds. But, as you can see below, the advantages aren't exclusive to investors in the highest tax brackets. A simple way to compare taxable and tax-free investments is to look at what your investment may yield after taxes. This is known as a taxable-equivalent yield comparison. The higher your tax bracket, the more a taxable investment, such as Treasuries or corporate bonds, would have to earn to equal a municipal bond's tax-free yield.

Example:

Consider a $100,000 taxable investment yielding 6%. For one year, you would have earned $6,000. But depending upon your federal tax bracket, you could have paid the following to Uncle Sam:

The Tax Dilemma[1]

28% Tax Rate: Paid $1,680 in taxes; Kept $4,320.

---

[1]   Interest from Municipal bonds may be subject to AMT.

33% Tax Rate: Paid $1,980 in taxes; Kept $4,020.

35% Tax Rate: Paid $2,100 in taxes; Kept $3,900.

The Tax-Free Alternative

The same $100,000 placed in a tax-free investment yielding 4.5% for one year would have earned $4,500— that would have been yours to keep in your account.

Investors are often surprised to learn that investments paying tax-free income can be more successful at building wealth than their typically higher-yielding, taxing cousins—corporate bonds and Treasury bonds. Not only is the income tax free, but those dollars, when reinvested, compound tax free as well. For this reason, a municipal bond account may be able to grow faster than a taxable bond account.

Tax-free income funds offer one of the easiest ways to take advantage of tax-free opportunities, while providing other benefits.

- Diversification: Tax-free mutual funds hold many different municipal bonds, which can help cushion the impact any one bond has on the overall portfolio value.
- Management: Professional managers devote their time and resources to analyzing opportunities and market conditions, so you don't have to.
- Monthly Dividends: While most individual municipal bonds only make semi-annual distributions, many tax-free mutual funds distribute dividend income monthly. You can choose to receive a monthly check, or reinvest your dividends to benefit from tax-free compounding.
- Accessibility and Convenience: Tax-free mutual funds offer you access to municipal bonds that may be expensive for you to purchase directly. Mutual funds also allow you to buy or sell shares daily, as well as make automatic

investments and withdrawals from your account on a monthly basis[2].

Investors need to keep in mind that the real return on their investment is the return they have left after they pay Uncle Sam and all his friends in the state and local tax collection offices. The difference between a 10% gain taxed at 36% (one of the highest income tax brackets) and a 10% gain taxed at a 15% (the highest long-term capital gains rate) is quite significant. While tax consequences should always be something you consider when investing, never let taxes be the tail that wags the investment dog. Conversely, lower income tax folks would be discouraged from buying tax-free bonds due to their unsuitability.

Funding retirement accounts can help keep your current income tax lower. Maximizing the amount of investing you do inside retirement accounts is generally a wise strategy. By doing so, you reduce the amount of your income currently taxable and shelter your investments' profits from taxation over time.

Some of the investing that you'll want to do, however, happens outside retirement accounts. But we want to stress that it is only after you've maxed out all the tax-sheltered retirement account possibilities, that you should consider other investments. So the type of non-retirement account investments that makes sense for you will depend at least partly on your tax situation.

Consider a nondeductible IRA only after you have exhausted the possibilities of contributing to retirement accounts that do provide an immediate tax deduction, such as 401(k)s, SEP-IRAs, Keoghs, and so on. If you've exhausted contributing to an IRA and still want to put away more money in retirement accounts, consider annuities, which are mutual fund investment contracts

---

[2]   With funds, taxable capital gains are distributed on at least an annual basis. In comparison to individual bonds, there is no maturity date and the principal amount will fluctuate. As with all funds, there are sales charges.

with sub-accounts that are backed by insurance companies. If you, the annuity holder (investor), should die during the so-called accumulation phase (that is, prior to receiving payments from the annuity), your designated beneficiary is guaranteed to be reimbursed the amount of your original investment or the maximum anniversary value. (See the specific details of the annuity. The features of the annuity vary widely with different insurance companies.)

Annuities, like IRAs, allow your capital to grow and compound tax-deferred. You defer taxes until withdrawal. However, unlike an IRA that has an annual contribution limit, you can deposit as much as you want in any year into an annuity—even a million dollars or more if you have it. As with any nondeductible IRA, you get no up-front tax deduction for your contributions. Annuities generally make sense if you have a longer period to invest and enjoy the tax deferral while insuring your investment to your beneficiaries. Annuities have been described as IRAs on steroids given their lack of any maximum lifetime contributions. It's important to note that annuities also incur sales charges and expenses not found in typical equity investments, and they may also have an early withdrawal period[3]

When considering investments, we want to remind you to always include the possible tax consequences in making your final decision. But tax considerations alone should not dictate how and where you invest your money. You should also weigh investment options, your desire (and the necessity) to take risk, personal likes and dislikes, and the number of years you plan to hold the investment.

Tax-Reduction Strategies Review List:

1. Up to certain limits, the money you put into an employer-sponsored retirement plan won't be included in your

---

[3] For details about annuities, or for an annuitiy prospectus, please feel free to contact my office.

taxable income that year, and many companies make matching contributions, giving your retirement fund an additional return. If you qualify for a tax-deductible IRA, contribute the maximum to help build your retirement savings.

2. If you own a home, you may want to convert nondeductible consumer interest to deductible interest. You can't deduct the interest you pay on credit cards, car loans, and other consumer loans. Refinancing these loans with a home equity loan may enable you to deduct the interest you pay. However, we urge you to use this strategy with extreme caution. You don't want to jeopardize your personal castle due to frivolous spending and expenses.

3. If you itemize on your tax returns, and we bet you do, charitable donations can be deducted from your income, subject to certain limitations. By donating appreciated property, you avoid capital gains taxes and the charity receives the full value of the asset. For cash donations over $250, you will need to be able to provide a receipt from the organization to claim a deduction. A canceled check is no longer enough proof.

4. Sadly, many taxpayers miss out on deductions simply because they keep careless records. Maintain a filing system throughout the year and keep receipts or other documentation of your deductible expenses. Be sure to keep documentation regarding purchase prices of investments in the same manner as you keep records of your home and home improvement projects. You'll need this information when you sell any of these assets.

5. If you are in a marginal tax bracket of 28% or higher, you can benefit from investments that produce long-term capital gains—which are taxed at a maximum rate of 15% (if held longer than 12 months).

📁 From The Real Life Files of Pat Vitucci
*The following is a real life example where the names have been
changed. But the situation described is accurate.*

Margie recently retired from a large Fortune 500 company
after a wonderful career of 37 years with the same firm. (This
scenario will become more rare in the future given the lack of
both company and employee loyalty.) Margie accumulated
$515,000 in her 401(k) by diligently contributing to her plan
over her tenure with the company. Her plan was diversified
because she checked with her financial advisor every couple of
quarters and redeployment decisions were executed with
regularity.

Margie is considering paying off the balance of her mortgage
($190,000 at 6.5%) with the proceeds from her 401(k), to provide
emotional relief from those monthly mortgage payments. She is
also preparing to take monthly checks from the balance of her
401(k) which is equal to 12% annually of her portfolio.

Pat Recommendations:

STOP! Hold Everything! After a long, rewarding, careful
career, Margie is about to make several serious blunders. Her
"emotional relief" that she is seeking will give her sleepless nights
unless she considers the ramifications of her decisions. By
withdrawing $190,000 from her pre-tax 401(k) plan, she will
immediately volunteer to add $190,000 to her current year's
income. Almost 50% of that withdrawal ($95,000) will be payable
to Uncle Sam via Federal and State taxes. Therefore, Margie will
effectively need to withdraw significantly more in order to net
$190,000.

Secondly, assuming a return of 12% annually from the balance
is unrealistic. Despite the 75 year track records of the equity

markets of 11% annually, we recommend a 7-1/2 % systematic withdrawal to accommodate future inflationary affects and other possible mitigating events in Margie's life. Erosion of her principal with a 12% withdrawal rate will guarantee her emotional UN-relief.

Key Points from Chapter 6:

1. Taking advantage of tax-deductible retirement accounts should be a financial priority.
2. Be sure your investment returns are beating inflation rates. Otherwise, you're losing money.
3. Keep careful records to see not only where your money goes, but also to track deductions.

7

Estate Planning

A billion here, a billion there, pretty soon it adds up to real money.—Senator Everett Dirksen

When you think "what if" we hope it is usually something pleasant—like "what if this is the year I win the marathon?" or "what if this year we vacation in Bora Bora?" Nobody likes to think, "What if my spouse is paralyzed or dies?" That may explain why so many people tend to overlook estate planning as part of their financial strategies. They just don't want to think about it. Yet, here you are reading this book and we hope you will think about it. Most people spend more time planning their vacations than they spend planning their estates.

Actually, you probably do care what happens to your affairs in the event of your incapacity or death. Fortunately, there are strategies you can use today to plan for the preservation and distribution of your wealth. An effective estate plan considers the creation, preservation, and distribution of your estate to maximize your family's welfare. It considers the effects of taxes, probate, property ownership, and a host of other issues.

There are five methods you can use to control the distribution of your estate:

Intestacy

If you die without a valid will, you die intestate. By doing nothing, you subject your heirs to a variety of complications:

- Distribution according to state law. Without a proper estate plan in place, the courts will have to rely on the intestacy laws of your state. Chances are they will not distribute your estate as you would have preferred. And the state has no particular concern for the best interest of you or your family.
- Fees and taxes. By dying intestate, you have done nothing to reduce or eliminate the administrative fees and estate taxes brought on as a result of your death. If your estate exceeds the estate tax exemption amount, estate taxes may be due.
- Probate. Without advanced planning, your estate will go through probate, which can be a time-consuming and costly process, one that your heirs may want to avoid.

Wills

The second way to control the distribution of your estate is to have a will drawn up. A will is simply a list of instructions that tells the probate court how you would like your estate distributed. Using a will enables you to control how your assets are distributed.

Because wills are essentially written instructions to the probate court, they ensure probate. And probate can have some significant drawbacks. Probate is the court-supervised proceedings that conclude all the legal and financial affairs of the deceased. Probate may take from six months to a year or even more. Your beneficiaries will probably have to wait until probate is concluded before they receive the assets you intended for them to have bequeathed to them. Probate can also be quite expensive. Depending on your state, probate and administrative fees can consume between 2 and 10% of your gross estate— before deducting mortgages, taxes, and other liens. Finally, the proceedings of the probate court are public record. Anyone can go to the county courthouse and find out exactly how much you owned, as well as how much you left and to whom. This will leave your heirs will little or no privacy.

Trusts

The third alternative, trusts, offers a way to avoid probate. In general, a trust is a three-party arrangement where the owner of a property—the trustor or grantor—transfers title of the property to a second party—the trustee—for the benefit of a third party— the beneficiary. The trustee is responsible for managing the property for the beneficiary, according to the terms spelled out in the trust agreement.

There are several types of trusts:

Living trusts are established and funded during your lifetime. Using a living trust can enable you to control distribution of your estate. Utilizing special types of living trusts may also allow you to minimize estate taxes that will be imposed upon your death. And living trusts completely avoid probate. The assets you place in a living trust will be available to your heirs, without the delays or expensive court proceedings that accompany the probate process.

Testamentary trusts are set up according to instructions in your will and take effect upon your death. A testamentary trust will enable you to control the distribution of your estate and may enable your estate to avoid unnecessary taxes upon the death of a second spouse. As testamentary trusts are usually established by your will, your assets will go through probate before they are transferred to the trust.

While testamentary trusts become irrevocable only upon your death, living trusts can be either revocable or irrevocable.

A revocable trust is a trust that you can alter or revoke at any time. It provides a measure of security because you know that it can change according to your needs. However, because you can alter or revoke them, revocable living trusts do not offer any estate tax benefits. They are used primarily for property management, asset protection, and probate avoidance.

An irrevocable trust is a trust that cannot be altered or revoked once it is established. An irrevocable trust provides many benefits of the revocable trust. In addition, it provides the potential for estate tax savings. Once property is transferred to an irrevocable trust, all future appreciation in value of that property will be excluded from your estate. This can help you minimize estate taxes. Just remember, once you set up an irrevocable trust, you cannot alter, amend, or revoke it.

Property Ownership

The fourth way of controlling the distribution of your estate is through property ownership. You can own property in your own name or you can own it jointly.

Contracts

Contracts are the final way you can control the distribution of your estate. If you own a life insurance policy, an annuity, an IRA, or if you have been participating in a company-sponsored retirement plan, you have named beneficiaries who will take title to these accounts upon your death. Because the contract specifies your chosen beneficiary, there is no need to probate the proceeds of the underlying account.

Estate Taxes

The estate tax is a tax on the right to transfer property. The government says that every American has the right to transfer up to an exempted amount without any estate tax liability. The government doesn't particularly care if you transfer property while you are living, in the form of gifts, or after you have died. You have one exempted package that you can transfer free of estate or gift taxes. If you are married, you and your spouse can each transfer this amount tax-free. This means that with careful attention to the legal ownership of assets, a couple can transfer twice the amount to their children, grandchildren, or anyone else, free of federal estate taxes. Once you go above the exemption amount, a highly progressive estate tax with rates as high as 55% comes into play.

If you have a sizable estate, the government wants a large share of it when you die. However, effective use of the unlimited martial deduction and the unified credit can help reduce these taxes. The federal government exempts most transfers of wealth between spouses from federal estate and gift taxes. Regardless of the size of an estate, no federal income taxes will be due when a husband or wife dies and leaves his or her wealth to the surviving spouse. There are some exceptions to this rule.

The unified credit is a special tax credit that can be used to reduce your estate taxes. This credit offsets your estate taxes dollar for dollar. That means that if the total value of your estate is less than the exemption amount, there will be no federal estate tax liability upon your death. Although a couple may be able to transfer an estate valued at twice the exemption amount free of federal estate taxes, the unified credit does not automatically allow them to do this. If you hold property jointly with your spouse, or if you have a simple will, you may only utilize the full unified credit when the second spouse passes away.

Relying on the unlimited marital deduction to avoid taxes upon the death of the first spouse will merely postpone taxes to the death of the surviving spouse. When the second spouse passes away, the estate tax burden may be unnecessarily large and your heirs' share of your estate may be unnecessarily small. But with planning, you can ensure that both you and your spouse benefit from the unified credit. Failing to plan ahead may result in more taxes.

To reduce the value of your estate, you may want to consider making gifts to family members. You can transfer up to $11,000 per person per year to as many recipients as you wish with no gift tax liability. If you are married, and your spouse consents, together you can make joint gifts of up to $22,000 per person per year. These limits are indexed for inflation. These gifts won't use up any of your estate tax exemption. The transfers must be present-interest gifts. The recipients must be able to use and enjoy the gift today. However, gifts of more than $11,000 are subject to gift taxes unless you use your unified credit to avoid paying them.

And remember, gifts don't have to be outright gifts of cash. For example, you can give assets with low current values and high appreciation potential. However, if the recipients sell the assets, they will incur capital gains based on your original costs and, therefore, incur a higher tax liability.

Charitable giving can provide many estate and income tax advantages to the giver. Within certain limits, a gift to charity can provide you with a charitable deduction for your income taxes. In addition, your gift will reduce your eventual estate tax liability.

Charitable remainder trusts enable you to reduce or avoid capital gains taxes on the sale of appreciated assets. To use a charitable remainder trust, you transfer appreciated property to an irrevocable trust and name your favorite charity as the eventual beneficiary. The appreciated property is then sold, and the proceeds are reinvested. You then receive income generated by the trust for the rest of your life. At the termination of the trust, the property passes to your chosen charity. Please note that not all charitable organizations are able to use all possible gifts. It is prudent to first check with the charity. The type of organization you select can also affect the tax benefit you receive. The charitable remainder trust strategy allows you to convert low-yielding, highly appreciated property into income-producing assets without triggering heavy taxes on your capital gains. And your eventual estate taxes may be reduced as well.

With a charitable lead trust, you transfer assets to a trust and give the charity an income interest in the property, so the charity earns income from the assets. At your death, the trust assets pass to your heirs, with potentially sizable savings on estate taxes. Besides reducing estate taxes, you may be able to take a current deduction for the present value of the charity's interest in your gift. Be careful—charitable trusts are irrevocable. Use them only if you're sure you won't need the asset.

Other Estate Planning Considerations

Although these don't necessarily reduce your estate taxes, the following considerations can be a valuable part of your estate plan. A durable power of attorney enables you to name a trusted individual to act on your behalf in the event you become incapacitated. With a durable power of attorney, this person can make financial and legal decisions that could affect your overall estate until such time as you recover.

A health care proxy is similar to a durable power of attorney in that it nominates a family member or other trusted individual to make decisions regarding your health care. It authorizes the person you select to make decisions regarding life support, funeral, and burial arrangements, in addition to other issues. While rules relating to a health care proxy vary from state to state, it can be a very valuable estate planning tool.

A living will is a legal document outlining your wishes about prolonging your life by artificial, extraordinary, or heroic measures. Living wills are most often used to authorize termination of life support in the event of a terminal illness. Like health care proxies, the rules regarding living wills differ according to the state in which you live. However, the personal nature of medical care in our technology advance world makes this planning tool important.

Finally, one of the big difficulties facing your heirs after your death will be locating all the relevant documents to help dispose of your estate in the manner you directed. Below we've listed some of the items you can use to create your own "personal document locator." A personal document locator will help you record the location of your valuable papers, assets, and other important items. As anyone who has faced the challenge of being the estate executor for a pack rat will tell you, "Please fill this out now!"

Personal Information

Name   Date _____

Residence Address

Office Address

Safe Deposit* Box #   Bank

Address

Personal Papers

Birth Certificate

Baptismal Certificate

Medical Records

Burial Records

Letters of Last Instruction

Other

Insurance Policies

Life

Disability

Health / Medical

Long-Term Health Care

Homeowner's

Other

Legal Documents
Marriage Certificate
Divorce Papers
Social Security Card(s)
Powers of Attorney
Will
Trust Agreement(s)
Veteran Papers
Health Care Proxy
Living Will
Other

Financial Documents
Mortgage Papers
Bank Account
Brokerage Account
Stock or Bond Certificates
Income Tax Returns
Gift Tax Returns
Employee Benefit Data
Other

Titles and Deeds
Automobile
House
Other Real Estate
Cemetery Plot
Other

Important People

Medical Doctor	Phone
Accountant	Phone
Attorney	Phone
Banker	Phone
Employer	Phone
Financial Advisor	Phone

Insurance Agent	Phone
Stockbroker	Phone
Other Phone	

Institutions

Bank (savings)	Account #
Bank (checking)	Account #
Credit Union	Account #
Money Market Fund	Account #
Other	

- Should you keep all your important documents in a safe deposit box? In a word—no! Safe deposit boxes are excellent for most important financial and legal documents, but there are some documents you shouldn't keep there. Keep your will and life insurance policies somewhere else. Generally, your safe deposit box will be locked upon your death—just when these important documents will be needed most.

- It is important to note that the services of a qualified estate planning attorney should be considered given the complex nature of the legal system. The authors are **NOT** attorneys, nor do they have a legal background or education.

📂 From The Real Life Files of Pat Vitucci
The following is a real life example where the names have been changed. But the situation described is accurate.

Sydney and Beatrice are both retired, ages 82 and 81, respectively, and have recently moved into an Assisted Living Facility after having lived in a retirement village for the last 12 years. Their health is declining and their two daughters have encouraged this move so that Mom and Dad can have more attention and care. Their estate is worth approximately $5 million and despite repeated discussions with their daughters; the parents have been reluctant to engage their services of an estate planning attorney. All of the assets of Sydney and Beatrice are held in joint accounts, except Sydney's IRA, which is held in his name with Beatrice as the beneficiary. Sydney and Beatrice live in California, which is a community property state.

Pat's Recommendation:

Sydney and Beatrice along with their two daughters should secure the services of a qualified estate planning attorney. Upon the death of Sydney and Beatrice and after the annual exclusions are applied, currently for 2004 at $1.5 million, the excess estate will be taxed to the daughters based on a tax table that is incremental up to a 55% tax bracket.

Additionally, Sydney's IRA, with Beatrice as the beneficiary, is proper, but contingent beneficiaries of the two daughters should be named to further the legacy of those IRA dollars. As contingent beneficiaries, the two daughters can enjoy those inherited IRA dollars over their life expectancies, based on IRA tables using their considerable younger ages. A myriad of other tax saving issues can be implemented based on properly executed legal documents.

Key Points from Chapter 7:

1. Determine the worse case scenario "what ifs" for your situation and then take steps to prevent them from creating financial disaster for you and your family.
2. The most caring legacy you can create is to have your estate in order for your loved ones.
3. Be sure that Uncle Sam is not the biggest beneficiary of your estate.

8

Selection of a Financial Advisor

Never spend your money before you have it.—Thomas Jefferson

The media pays an awful lot of attention to the market, though quite often it only looks at a particular index (such as the Dow) and considers that representative of the market as a whole. The market is considered to be bullish if it is going up, bearish if it going down and volatile if it is scooting up and down in quick succession. But what if you don't want, or have the time, to watch the market ticker every day? If not, we suggest you outsource, of course.

As Harry Dent points out in his book, *The Roaring 2000s,* "Financial planners and advisors are emerging in the investment industry to coordinate a one-stop financial investment system for individuals. They can coordinate all aspects of a customized financial plan, especially for busy professionals who have little time." (p. 144)

A financial advisor is a licensed professional who can work with you in creating a blueprint for your investments to build a path for reaching your goals. But with your hard-earned dollars and retirement at stake, how do you choose a "good one?"

Let's start with a few red flags for you to watch out for:

1. An advisor who doesn't listen. Before you hire a financial pro, you should know precisely what questions you want answered—and what you're paying for—before you write that first check. It should be a two-way effort, with both of you probing for a good fit. In particular, when you ask questions, do you understand the answers? When you ask for clarification, does the subsequent explanation make more sense? Are you comfortable admitting you don't understand something? Be wary of somebody who either desperately wants your business or can't "lower themselves" to your level.

2. "Please sign here. I'll explain later." It goes without saying, but we wish to repeat something you've heard before: Don't sign anything that you don't understand. Don't write out checks directly to the planner for financial products and investments. Most importantly, don't sign a "discretionary authority" unless you know exactly what you are doing. This enables a planner to buy and sell investment without consulting you ahead of time. Granted, there are many cases where you want to take advantage of this feature. But, again—be sure you understand.

3. Amateurs masquerading as pros. It pays to check up on professional credentials, and can save you a few calls to the Better Business Bureau before it's too late. Don't rely on the titles. Even the shadiest of characters is free to use it too. What if the individual provider or firm principal is not registered with SEC or the state securities agency? We want to advise you to always, always work with a National Association of Securities

Dealers (NASD) member. Proceed to the nearest exit if they are not NASD members.

4. Advice you don't need. Unless you are specifically looking for stock picks, be wary of an advisor who is preoccupied with them, especially if they generate commission income by getting you to actively trade. Good advisors always put the basics—like insurance and cash flow—before investment advice, and all specific investment recommendation should fit into a larger framework built around your financial goals. Any discussion of investments should involve risk. If an advisor promotes any investment as a risk-free "sure thing," or offers you "exclusive access," find another advisor, especially if the promised reward is very attractive. Our experience is that this is another disguise for "to good to be true."

5. That churning-gut feeling. Do you trust your right-hand man or woman's advice? You're paying for it, you should. If you're wary, then maybe your gut instincts are telling you something about your level of trust. If your advisor's guidance makes sense, make sure you follow it—you paid good money for it, after all. As many have argued, procrastination plays a leading role in economics. So, if your advisor says you need to open a Roth IRA and you agree then do it. Not doing so is a waste of your money.

The investment field is filled with a lot of jargon. There are literally tens of thousands of different investments. Unfortunately, for the novice, and even for experts who will be honest with you, the names of the investments are just the tip of the iceberg. Underneath each of investments lurks a veritable mountain of details. If you wanted to and had the time, you could make a full-time endeavor out of analyzing financial statements, talking to the business's employees, customers, suppliers, and so on. That why you must be realistic and selective about choosing investments—if you're like most of us, you have a limited time on Earth.

Making wise investments need not take a lot of your time. If you know where to get high-quality information and purchase good, managed investments, you can do the things that you're best at and have more free time for the fun things in life. An important part of this process of choosing wise investments, we hope, will be knowing when to hire others to help you. For example, when investing in foreign stock markets, it makes far more sense to hire a good money manager, such as through a mutual fund, rather than going to all the time, trouble, and expense of trying to pick individual stocks on your own.

We'd like to discuss the reasons why you should choose a fee-based advisor versus a commission-based advisor. First, let's define the terms and their motivations. A commission-based advisor is someone who is generally limited to only a few propriety products that he will receive a commission on when he sells them. This type of advisor does not offer advice other than to urge you to purchase the "hot investment" he's selling. Generally speaking, he isn't interested in helping you build a well-balanced portfolio to reach your investment goals. The only way you will see him again is when he remembers to call you to sell you the next "hot investment." Your goal is to increase your money by investing in long-term assets. His only goal is to convince you to part with your hard-earned dollars on an asset that he will definitely make money on (his commission), when it may or may not be the right investment for your goals. If money is not moving, the proverbial commission cash register is not ringing. Money in motion is the goal of a commission based product sales person.

A recent report documented that 85% of financial planners earn most of their income from commissions from products that they sell. The small number of fee-based advisors has traditionally been for the affluent. But with the recent shifts in the industry, that too is changing, and for the benefit of investors. This inability to find objective financial help in the past has been all the more frustrating as individuals face increasingly complex choices. More employees are being forced to take responsibility for saving money for their retirement and deciding how to invest it.

A fee-based advisor is of a completely different mindset than the commission-based advisor. He is interested in helping you create a well-balanced portfolio. He will take the time to discuss not just what your goals are, but your risk tolerance, your time horizon, and review your entire financial picture. With a fee-based advisor you can be assured that he is offering you investments that provide both of you with the same goal. Since he is paid a percentage per year (generally 1-2%) of your assets, it is in his best interest and yours for those assets to grow and increase in value.

For example:

If you invest $100,000 with him, he would earn $1,500 if his fee is 1.5% per year. So since you both want the same goal, for the money to grow, you can truly work together.

Plus, you can easily see that a fee-based advisor is a dedicated professional that is committed to assisting you in reaching goals, not just looking for the next sale without ever looking reflecting on recent investment decisions. In a fee-based program, motivations of clients and advisors coincide perfectly. Clients want values to increase, advisors want values to increase. It is a win-win relationship, not a win-lose relationship.

"But wait!" you say, what about doing this online by yourself? Online trading has exploded over the past few years. That's great for technically inclined folks, but is it right for you? Yes, there is a plethora of articles out there in the wild Web about finance. The short length of these articles can easily lead writers to oversimplify complex issues. For example, many of these pieces focus mostly on past returns and company philosophies. Little, if any, space is devoted to the risks or tax consequences of investing in the recommended investments. Are you truly interested, or able, to do the diligent investigating, research, and analyzing for yourself? The analogy can be made that sure you can cut your own hair, but do you really want to? And then willingly appear out in public? We didn't think so.

If you're in a domestic relationship, you must both go to see the advisor. Before you do, we urge you and your partner to have a talk about what you want to accomplish with the advisor and the fears about money you have and make sure you both have a thorough understanding of where you stand right now. After you've chosen an advisor, you must make all decisions as a team and both be kept up-to-date with what the advisor is doing.

We see many clients, women in particular, who are financially overwhelmed when their husband dies or when they go through a painful separation or divorce. We've also seen how bewildered many people are when their parents die, leaving them an inheritance. When you have suffered a loss, you are in a state of grief, and this is not the time to make major financial decisions.

If you and your spouse are interviewing an advisor together, you must both feel comfortable talking to him intimately about your money. The advisor should address you both equally, give you plenty of time, and answer your questions, plus explain fees in a way you can easily understand. You should also be comfortable with the kinds of investments he suggests and understand everything about them when he explains them to you. If he fails to meet any of these criteria, keep shopping for another advisor.

Here are a few expectations you should have for a prospective financial advisor:

- That he will call you every time she makes a change in your account, unless you have a Registered Investment Advisor.
- That he will explain in thorough detail why he wants you to make every new transaction.
- That he will tell you without you having to ask if he is selling you something that isn't in your retirement account. And then explain the full tax consequences possible from this investment.
- That he will never pressure you into doing anything which doesn't feel right for you.

- That he will send you a transaction slip confirmation from the brokerage firm that holds your money, telling you what's been bought or sold. This slip must always match the transactions you gave permission for purchase or sale.
- That he will send you a quarterly statement summarizing all that quarter's transactions and informing you of the exact return he is getting on your money, as well as all fees. These reports should also show you all the realized gains or losses and all the unrealized gains or losses. These reports should also include returns of the overall index, so you know whether you're doing worse or better than the index.
- That he will return your calls in a timely manner.
- That he will keep you informed about your money, not just call you when he wants to sell you something.
- Finally, he should never ask you to write a check made out to him personally. Instead, all checks need to be made payable to the institution. This is absolutely essential.

Many people contact our office telling us just one fact and one fact only about their lives: how much they have to invest. This tells us nothing about them, and nothing about their financial situation. If someone says he has $10,000 to invest, but also has a credit card debt of $8,000 at 18%, it may be that his best investment of all would be to pay off that debt first. If someone is going to be looking after and investing your money, that person should know everything in your financial life, including how you feel about risks and about your goals.

When you go to interview financial advisors, you are considering whether you want to hire each one. Don't lose sight of the fact that you're the boss. You are ultimately in charge of your money and when you hire someone to take care of it—just as when you hire a qualified nanny for your children—you are the boss of that person as well. What the two of you need to build is a responsible, respectful, and trusting relationship. Please don't settle for anything less.

No matter where you seek financial advice, and we encourage you to use a financial advisor, remember that it is your money—and you are an at-will customer. In the end, you call the shots. If you encounter a third party who insists that you relinquish all the thinking to them, then we humbly suggest that this may not be the best pro for you.

We'd like to leave you with an outline of items a competent financial planner can assist you with:

1. Identify problems and goals. Many otherwise intelligent people have a hard time being objective about their financial problems. They may ignore their debts or have unrealistic goals and expectations given their financial situations and behaviors. Also, many are so busy with other aspects of their lives that they never take the time to think about what their financial goals are. A good financial advisor can give you the objective look you need.

2. Identifying strategies to reach your financial goals. Your mind may be a jumble of various plans, ideas, and concerns, along with a cobweb or two. A good counselor can help you sort out your thoughts and can propose alternative strategies for you to consider in accomplishing your financial goals.

3. Setting priorities. You could be doing a dozen things to improve your financial situation, but making a few key changes could probably have the greatest value. Equally important is to identify the changes that fit your overall situation and that won't keep you awake at night fretting about them. Good planners help you prioritize.

4. Saving research time and hassle. Even if you know what major financial decisions are most important to you, doing the research can be time-consuming and frustrating if you don't know where to turn for good information and advice. A good planner does research to match your needs to the best available strategies and products. There is so much poor and misleading information printed on financial topics

that you can easily get lost, discouraged, sidetracked or swindled. A good advisor can prevent you from making a bad decision based on poor or insufficient information.

5. Providing an objective voice for major decisions. Deciding when to retire, how much to spend on a home purchase, and where to invest your money are big decisions. Getting swept up in the emotions of these issues can cloud your perspective and objectivity. A competent and sensitive advisor can cut through this cloud to raise issues and provide sound counsel.

6. Helping you to just do it. Deciding what you need to do is not enough—you have to actually do it, too. And although you can use a planner for advice and make all the changes on your own, a good counselor can help you follow through with your plan as well. After all, part of the reason you hired the advisor in the first place may be that you're too busy or uninterested to manage your finances.

7. Mediating. If you have a spouse or partner, financial decisions can produce real fireworks, particularly with financial decisions involving the extended family. Although a counselor can't be a therapist, a good one can be sensitive to the different needs and concerns of each party and can try to find a middle ground on the financial issues you're grabbling with.

8. Making you money and allowing you peace of mind. The whole point of professional financial planning is to help you make the most of your money and help you plan for and attain your financial and personal goals. In the process, the financial planner should show you how to enhance your investment returns; reduce your spending, taxes, and insurance costs; increase your savings; improve your catastrophic insurance coverage; and achieve your financial independence goals. And last but not least: Putting your financial house in order should take some weight off your mind.

📁 From The Real Life Files of Pat Vitucci
The following is a real life example where the names have been
changed. But the situation described is accurate.

Eugene retired at the age of 62 on December 31, 1999. He
worked for a lot of the last century but did not want to spend time
in this century as a working person. Congratulations to Eugene
after 40 years in the work force! Eugene was determined to control
his 401(k) so he went to his local bank branch and gave them
permission to rollover his 401(k) into a self-directed IRA. The
securities person in the bank's main lobby area was very
accommodating, probably given the fact that the rollover amounted
to $750,000. The rollover arrived at the bank approximately seven
weeks later, with a deposit date of February 20, 2000. The
commission based bank employee selected his bank's proprietary
investment options (these are called proprietary given that the
monies are managed by the bank's employees), and diversified
the $750,000 into four different proprietary investments. This was
a very aggressive posture but bear in mind that the five preceding
years in the stock market were quite attractive. Eugene did not
want to be left behind given all the excitement in the stock market.
The securities person at the bank indicated that he would monitor
the investment choices and communicate regularly with Eugene.
It was a big commission pay day for the bank employee.

As history has recorded, March 2000 was the peak of the
stock market, and for the next three years the market fell
precipitously. By mid-year 2000, the bank person that Eugene
was dealing with left the bank for other opportunities. Susan was
the new "rookie" now assigned to Eugene as well as responsible
for four other branches of the Big Bank; like her predecessor.
Susan is seated at a different branch of the bank each work day.
Susan did not have the opportunity to call Eugene until December
2000, when she had to deliver the bad news that his IRA's current

market value was $600,000, a 20% loss. Eugene was not monitoring his investment—given his new leisure lifestyle. Susan reassured Eugene that 2001 would be a recovery year and therefore did not make any re-allocations in Eugene's portfolio. One year later, Eugene called the bank and was informed that Susan had left the bank in April of 2001, but Benjamin would be calling soon for a review. In February 2002, Benjamin (another rookie recently licensed) delivered the bad news; Eugene's portfolio was now worth $480,000 and that his monthly check would necessarily have to be cut in half. This was quite a shock to Eugene and he walked out of the bank in despair.

Pat's Recommendation:

Unfortunately, Eugene volunteered for the investment philosophy of "INVEST AND FORGET." Because the employee was a "captive" bank employee, he was required to use the Big Bank's own investments and did not have the liberty of selecting among all of the other investment choices in the market. Secondly, and perhaps more importantly, the original licensed securities person enjoyed a nice commission pay day; there was not a method or procedure in place to provide the continuity of money management based on an ever-changing volatile economy. As market conditions changed over the period of the time, no adjustments were implemented. Stock market positions became increasingly more unattractive as fixed income investments' performances improved. An active asset allocation system that is fee based would have provided an incentive for the bank employee that matches perfectly with Eugene's. A fixed percentage of 1.5% of assets under management provides a motivational system that yields a win-win environment. Case in point: 1.5% of $750,000 is nice, but 1.5% of $850,000 is even more attractive. In this instance, each party is motivated to have the account grow. Also, select an advisor with an entire team of qualified professionals educated in modern portfolio theories of money management. A Certified Financial Analyst (CFA) is a difficult credential to achieve, but establishes a level of maturity and experience in this industry that should not be overlooked. An effective team effort should retain the services of one or more CFA's. Repositioning of Eugene's assets would have potentially retained a much larger portion of Eugene's portfolio.

Key Points from Chapter 8:

1. Work with a fee-based financial advisor who you feel comfortable with and who shares your investment temperament.
2. Diversify your portfolio and review it often. Remember our motto: DON'T INVEST AND FORGET.
3. Be sure that you understand all investments you make and know what risks are involved.

9

Monitoring Your Portfolio Regularly

Money is the opposite of the weather. Nobody talks about it,
but everybody does something about it.—Rebecca Johnson

Most important of all to the long-term success of your investment portfolio is paying attention. Diane Sawyer once commented, "The greatest lesson I ever learned was to pay attention." Not bad advice from an award-winning news reporter. Would you buy a plant and never water it? Would you buy a dog and let him keep eating the curtains after you're explicitly and patiently explained the reasons he shouldn't? Well of course not. The same is true, for a portfolio of investments. All investment portfolios need to be checked up on a regular basis to see if it is matching or beating the market indexes.

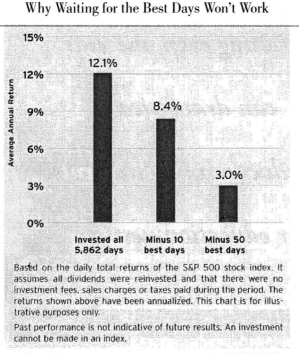

Why Waiting for the Best Days Won't Work

Based on the daily total returns of the S&P 500 stock index. It assumes all dividends were reinvested and that there were no investment fees, sales charges or taxes paid during the period. The returns shown above have been annualized. This chart is for illustrative purposes only.

Past performance is not indicative of future results. An investment cannot be made in an index.

*1987-2003

Reviewing your investments, particularly when you may have made mistakes, offers a crucial opportunity to learn from your mistakes rather than being doomed to repeat them. Everyone makes errors on occasion, but most successful investors avoid making the same errors more than once. Set aside time to review your portfolio, preferably every month, or at least every three months when you receive your quarterly statement. We suggest when you get your quarterly reports to not just open the envelope and file the papers, but to actually read through them. You'd be surprised how many people don't read their statements. While we are not recommending that you glue yourself to your computer and check on your assets minute-by-minute; tossing your quarterly statements in a drawer and forgetting them is not a great plan either.

As Robert Hagstrom, Jr. writes, in *The Warren Buffett Way*, "the traditional yardstick for measuring performance is price change: the difference between the purchase price of the stock and the market price of the stock. In the long run, the price of a stock should approximate the change in value of the business. However, in the short run, prices can gyrate widely above and below a company's value, dependent on factors other than the progress of the business. The problem remains that most investors use short-term changes to gauge the success of failure of their investment approach. However, these short-term price changes often have little to do with the changing economic value of the business and much to do with anticipating the behavior of other investors.

"Frequently, clients become impatient while waiting for the price of their portfolio to advance at some predetermined rate. If their portfolios do not show short-term performance gains, clients become dissatisfied and skeptical of the investment professional's ability. Knowing that they must improve short-term performance or risk losing clients, professional investors become obsessed with chasing stock prices." (p. 80)

So if even a financial wizard like Warren Buffett invests and views his billion dollar portfolio for the long-term—there is a lesson for the rest of us to learn as well. In the planned review of your investment statements and results, take this lesson to heart. Knowing that the market resembles a roller coaster at times, take a step back so that you can see the Big Picture of your investments.

It is very important to learn to accept that your money will have its ups and downs. No matter how carefully you plan— even if you do every financial lesson well—money, like every other aspect of life, isn't always going to behave in ways you can predict. Sometimes you'll have more than you expected, and at other times, money will flow out and you'll have less than you thought. There may be a time when you have money in the stock market and it goes down dramatically. Or maybe you suddenly inherit a valuable piece of property. Perhaps you get downsized from your job without warning—or given a surprise promotion. We've seen this ebb and flow with our clients time and time again.

You think your financial life is rolling along a certain track and wham! You're going in a different direction.

Five Ways to Focus on the Big Picture

If you want to go forward, try taking a step back to allow you room to look at the big picture. Too many investors get lost in the details. Here are five critical issues.

1. **Your Goals:** Suppose you want to send the kids to a ritzy private college. That's an admirable goal. But it probably won't happen, unless you make it a financial priority.
2. **Your Portfolio Mix:** Many folks never consciously settle on target percentages for stocks and investments. The result is that these folks may be taking far too little risk— or way too much.
3. **Your Tax Bracket:** Your tax bracket is crucial as you weigh whether to fund a regular individual retirement account or a Roth IRA. Whenever you make an investment decision, you should think about the tax consequences.
4. **Your Financial Risks:** Consider the costs of life's truly devastating losses. Tally what the financial risks are if your house burns down, totaling your car, getting sued, suffering a disability, or the death of the family breadwinner. Don't overdo it; but also we don't want you facing financial ruin because of it.
5. **Your Life Expectancy:** It's not fun to contemplate how long you're going to live. But it is important to realistically look at how long of a retirement you'll need to provide for.

These transitions can be exciting, or as if often the case scary, but they are all part of the natural cycle of life and money. So, we want to remind you to take a long view of your financial future. If you follow our outline, the setbacks you may have today or next year will not keep you from reaching your financial goals.

You've heard it said that when you first have a dream for yourself, you think it's totally impossible. As time goes on, you'll think it's highly improbable. In the end, you will know that it was attainable all along. But with your investments, it is not only prudent, but essential that you pay attention to them. DON'T INVEST AND FORGET.

We tend to meet three levels of investors, who are all trying to reach their goals. Each has a plan and each has its own reasons for choosing his investment choice. Perhaps you fall into one of these three levels. One of our goals of this book would be to assist you in achieving the highest level possible. Allow us to explain:

Level 1 Investor

Jeff is what we would typecast as a "Level 1 Investor." Jeff has always had a fascination with toothpaste. As you might expect, Jeff is a successful dentist who loves his work and takes great care with his clients. Jeff is a very gentle dentist and seeks out dental conventions for his vacation time every year. He's quite dedicated to his profession. Since Jeff has a love of toothpaste, he thought he should put his investment money into the stock of his favorite toothpaste manufacturer. Jeff didn't know much about the company, but he did know that he liked the toothpaste and recommended it to all of his clients. Sadly, the toothpaste manufacturer missed out on a new and improved whitening compound and suffered some big losses during the last couple of years. Jeff never seems to have the time to open his copy of the toothpaste company's annual report or review his stock's value. Jeff isn't sure how his company is performing relative to their competitors in the industry. He may be surprised to find out that the company's debt load at high percent bond interest rates are about to come due and their new marketing promotions are not producing desired results. So, when Wall Street industry analysts digest all this potential bad news, the stocks price may drop precipitously.

Consequently, Jeff is relying on superficial information for his decision making process of stock selection. Also, Jeff is missing out on diversifying his investment money. When the toothpaste manufacturer suffers a loss or enjoys a gain, Jeff's money fluctuates in the same manner. He has no protection from changes to the toothpaste industry, which the company he is invested with may or may not keep up with the industry fluctuations. To be an effective Level 1 Investor, Jeff needs to review many variables on a regular basis to carefully monitor his investment.

Level 2 Investor

Sean is what we would typecast as a "Level 2 Investor." Sean rides the train to work every day and overheard some other passengers talking about mutual funds. Sean is a busy fourth-grade teacher who spends his work days with 20 active children and their multitude of questions, problems, and recess games. A couple of days later on the way home from school, Sean picked up a popular financial advice magazine and noticed that they had a big cover article on "The Best Mutual Fund for You." Sean called the 800 number listed for the mutual fund and after filling out the form they faxed over to him, he wrote a large check to start his investment. Sean felt so great that he was finally "in the market" and was sure that his retirement would be fabulous. With his busy, hectic days Sean is usually overwhelmed at night and just grading papers, creating lesson plans, and enjoying his garden takes up most of his time. Sean notices his quarterly report from the mutual fund company, but he isn't quite sure what it means. But he has all of them saved in a box in the hallway closet. Sean may be interested in the fact that the star analyst with an excellent record of stock picking was recently pirated to a competing fund company. And a rookie will now be assuming that leadership position at the fund company.

Sean has diversified his money somewhat better than Jeff. However, Sean too isn't protected from market risk. Especially if the mutual fund Sean has joined is heavily invested in a speculative sector. Sean's risk tolerance and investment goals are immaterial to the mutual fund manager. The mutual fund may or may not be the right one for him. Sean must also understand that the analysts managing that specific fund must adhere to the fund objective. In other words, a Large Cap Fund (large company fund) must maintain 100% of its dollars invested in large companies, as defined by their filing submission to the NASD and SEC. The analysts can not compromise that fund objective by purchasing, for example, bonds, or utilities, or real estate, or any other asset, except large company stocks. If market conditions change and large company stocks fall out of favor and other market segments begin to look more attractive, that fund can not dilute its focus. That fund manager has no choice but to remain fully invested and watch the value of his fund drop. This adherence to the fund objective applies to ALL funds with a variety of different objectives (i.e. Bonds, Utilities, Mortgages, Real Estate, International, etc.) Therefore, it is intrinsic on Sean to monitor the various fund objectives and prospectively adjust his portfolio accordingly.

Level 3 Investor

Anita is what we lovingly refer to as a "Level 3 Investor." Anita owns a yarn store and gives knitting instruction classes each Tuesday evening. Anita inherited $129,000 from her father's estate last year and knew that she needed assistance in managing this new sum of money. Anita felt this would be a great start towards her retirement goals. Anita's investment portfolio is well diversified and appropriate to her risk tolerance level. She has also agreed to have her portfolio asset allocated, as needed, to keep her in alignment with market changes. Anita has hired a fee-based financial advisor with a full team of analysts who come to work every day and monitor approximately 100 indices[1].

Such as: Gross Domestic Product
            Consumer Price Index
            Housing Starts
            Interest Rates
            Confidence Index
            Sentiment Index
            Federal Reserve's Current Monetary Policy
            Political Environment
            . . . and so forth

As market conditions lean positively or negatively, adjustments are made to Anita's portfolio and she receives a confirmation of those adjustments in the mail. These confirmations reinforce Anita's decision that her very busy schedule did warrant delegating that function; and she is comforted knowing that her portfolio is being reviewed and adjusted with regularity.

Each quarter Anita receives a detailed report that outlines all of her assets, along with their values, as well as, her financial advisor's fees. Once a year, Anita meets with her financial advisor for a client review to be sure she's still on track to achieve her financial goals. Anita has been quite open to learning more about the stock market, but with her busy schedule, she delegates the day-to-day handling of her account to her financial advisor. Anita shopped around until she found someone who listened to her and who explained all her options. Anita feels confident that she will be able to retire and live in Hawaii, near the beach.

Anita has not only diversified her money, but also examined her risk tolerance and reviewed her investment goals. Anita has taken the time to educate herself on how her money is allocated. Anita is in a position to not only potentially grow her investment

---

[1]   There is no guarantee that a diversified portfolio will outperform a non diversified portfolio in any given market environment.

wisely, but will be able to make educated decisions about her financial life.

Yes, these three examples are somewhat over-simplifications of what we've encountered, but not by much. As you can see as investors move from "Level 1" to "Level 2" and onto "Level 3" their diversification increases as well as how their portfolio will adjust to the ever-changing market conditions[14]. Jeff and Sean are currently setting themselves up to invest and forget. Sadly, it doesn't need to be this way for either of these two guys. Both are intelligent and have the right idea—they need to invest for retirement. But both are missing out on great opportunities in the market, and both are not taking advantage of working with a professional advisor who can assist them in making the right choices for their personal portfolio. An effective financial advisor is someone you can form a trusting, respectful relationship, and delegate the day-to-day monitoring of your portfolio to follow your financial life.

Another one of the major difference between the levels is that "Level 3" utilizes asset allocation. A simple definition for asset allocation is the process of transferring your money from one investment asset to another in regards to changes to the current market situation. Think of your portfolio as a peach pie for dessert at a family dinner. Aunt Jayne only wants a sliver (she's on another diet). Uncle Ted wants a big piece—he loves peach pie. Your brother Pete says he'd like just a regular piece. And then your cousin Darren wants a regular piece but also a scoop of vanilla ice cream. You see, everyone chose a different portion. Next week, everyone's portion size could change based on the type of pie, what else they had for dinner, and how their diet's going. Just like in the market. One month you might want to have a big slice of small cap stocks, and next month you might want a tiny sliver.

Over time, asset allocation does more than manage risk—it can potentially boost returns. Consider the scenario of placing a $500 bet on one number of a roulette spin, as compared with

---

[14]   Diversification does not ensure against loss.

placing $25 on twenty different numbers. While the $500 may give a much better payoff, it also involves much more risk. The expected return on either bet is the same but the range of potential actual returns is better with the diversified bet.

Asset allocation was the basis for the Nobel prize-winning Modern Portfolio Theory (MPT) advanced by Harry Markowitz in 1990. MPT offers a different approach to investing by approaching the market through the holistic construction of a portfolio diversified among asset classes rather than employing fundamental analysis to traditional stock picking. MPT offers a method to determine suitable levels of risk for investors and then, based upon their personal tolerance for risk, to align them with investments that hold the most promise for investment return. Importantly, MPT found that diversification can reduce volatility[15]. The volatility of a diversified portfolio is less than the average of the volatilities of its component parts.

The more years you have to invest, the greater the difference a few percentage points will make on your returns. Let's show you some numbers.

If you invest $10,000 for 25 years or 40 years:

Rate of Return	In 25 Years, You'll Have	In 40 Years, You'll Have
4%	$26,658	$48,010
5%	$33,863	$70,399
10%	$108,347	$452,592

*This information is for illustrative purposes only and is not indicative of any specific investment

The goal we recommend to each of our clients is to have your portfolio managed and actively reviewed. You've heard us say it before, and we'll say it again: DON'T INVEST AND FORGET. You worked very hard for those precious dollars. Be sure you know where and how your money is working for you.

---

[15] Diversification does not ensure against loss.

As Harry Dent reminds us, "Successful investing is a lot like diet and exercise. Everybody knows what to do, but almost no one does it. Given a choice between eating broccoli or chocolate cake, we'll choose the chocolate cake every time, even though we know the broccoli is better for us. Broccoli is boring. Well, investing for the long term is equally boring. But are gambling and the excitement of beating the odds worth it? It is wise when your future, your retirement, your kid's education, and your ability to do what you really want with your life are at stake? If the answer is yes, maybe you should set aside some money every year and spend it at the crap tables in Las Vegas. The odds are better and at least you'll know you are gambling!" (p. 280)

Key Points from Chapter 9:

1. Regularly monitor your portfolio and make adjustments according to market changes.
2. Become a "Level 3 Investor" with a diversified portfolio that is professionally managed.
3. DON'T INVEST AND FORGET.

10

Your Budget in Retirement

Money is like a sixth sense without which you cannot make a complete use of the other five.—*W. Somerset Maugham*

M any people toil away at work, dreaming about a future in which they can stop the daily commute grind; get out from under that daily deluge of faxes, voice mails, and e-mails; and do what they want when they want. People often assume that this magical day will arrive either on their next true day off or when they retire or win the lottery, whichever comes first.

Part of the American dream is to be able to retire sooner rather than later. But this idea has some obvious problems. First, you set yourself up for disappointment. If you want to retire by your mid-60s, you'll need enough money to live for an additional 20 years, maybe longer. Two decades is a long time to live off your savings. You're going to need a good-sized chunk—more than most people realize. The earlier you hope to retire, the more money you need to set aside and the earlier you have to start saving.

In the past, more employers offered pension plans. In these plans, the employer set aside money on behalf of employees and retained a pension manager to decide how to invest it. The only responsibility of employees had to do was to determine what level of benefits they had earned and when they could begin drawing a monthly check. With today's plans, employees need to be educated about how much they to save and invest it. In addition to becoming a retirement planner and investment allocation, consumers face a dizzying number of financial products, that are marketed and distributed directly to consumers.

Two-thirds of all the men and women who have ever lived past 65 in the entire history of the world are alive today. Amazing! Thanks to the advances by the medical community, our awareness of health risks, and the increases in technology to ease our work load—we can all enjoy the prospect of a long life. Research is now indicating that the biological potential of the human body is believed to be somewhere between 120 and 140 years[1].

In 1975, a study was conducted with 3,000 people who were polled with the question, "How old is old?" The average answer was 65. Recently, a similar study was conducted by Dr. Ken Dychtwald in conjunction with AIG/SunAmerica Securities asking the same question. The overwhelming answer this time was 82. Quite dramatically, our perception of age has changed significantly in a relatively short time period. The big looming question to ask now is this "Is your financial life prepared for this potentially longer life?"

How "Old" is Old?

To illustrate the difference in our perception of aging, consider the following:

When Whistler painted his famous black and white depiction his mother sitting in a rocking chair, she was 65 years old. Recently, the lovely international movie actress

---

[1]   Revisioning Retirement, Dr. Ken Dychwald.

Sophia Loren celebrated her 65th birthday. These two women vividly demonstrate the changes on how we now look at aging.

Between 1946 and 1964, 76 million babies were born—that equaled one-third of the total population of America. Now those "baby boomers" are beginning to embark upon middle age and the start of their golden years. They are creating an evolution of the term retirement. Consider these facts[1]:

- In 1900, the average time spent in retirement was 1.2 years. Today, retirement averages over 19 years.
- In 1900, two out of three men 65 or older worked. By the end of the century, less than one in five were in the labor force.
- 85% of the U.S. population currently retires before their 65th birthday.
- While 65% of people save money for retirement, only 39% actually have tried to calculate how much money they need to save for retirement.
- The average 65-year old today can expect to live for another 19 years, compared with about 13 years for a 65-year old in 1940.
- By the year 2030, there will be 70 million people age 65 and older, more than twice the population for that age group in 2000. (U.S. Bureau of Labor Statistics)

Recently, AIG SunAmerica Securities completed an exhaustive study in conjunction with Dr. Ken Dychtwald on the "Re-Visioning of Retirement." They concluded that there are four distinct groups in retirement:

27% were termed "Ageless Explorers."

This active, energetic group felt youthful, empowered, and optimistic about their future. They are extremely happy, and love the freedom retirement has given them. Not surprisingly, this group boasts a high personal net worth and has invested wisely for their retirement.

19% were grouped as "Comfortably Contents."

These folks are living their golden years and are enjoying the fruits of their labors. They want to relax and play, while seeking freedom from work and responsibility. They too can boast a high personal net worth.

22% were called "Live for Todays."

Adventuresome and wanting to have fun best describes this segment. They had pursued active lives and personal growth. Overall, they are financially unprepared and have many regrets regarding their retirement. Their primary worry is that they will not have enough money saved. As you can imagine, this crowd has only a modest personal net worth.

32% were clustered in the "Sick and Tireds."

This group is populated by inactive, unfulfilled pessimists who are worried about everything. They are, understandably, the least happy and have given up. Their retirement has become a nightmare for them and, as expected, they have a low personal net worth.

After seeing what could be ahead, just as the ghost of Christmas future points out in Charles Dicken's famous tale, now is the time to take advantage of a financial wake-up call. The study also revealed that half of all baby boomer households currently have a total net worth of less than $10,000. The more years spent planning and preparing for retirement, the higher the level of satisfaction.

What Contributes Most to a Long Life?

47%	Supportive Friends and Family
46%	Strong Religious and Spiritual Beliefs
28%	Physical Activity
27%	Remaining Productive
12%	Goals and Aspirations
11%	Strong Finances
9%	Intellectual Stimulation

Financially liberated retirees have several common traits. They think positively towards their retirement, and see it as a continuance of life or a whole new adventure. They desire and achieve their active goals. These retirees participate in physical and intellectual activities, while seeking personal growth. Finally, they started saving early and developed an overall investment strategy. They also took advantage of professional assistance with a broad range of investment options.

The first step is retirement planning is calculating the cost of your retirement years. Remember that the costs of food, travel, entertainment, and medical treatment don't go down when you retire. In fact, they typically go up. Experts estimate that you'll need about 75% of your pre-retirement income to maintain a comfortable lifestyle. Inflation will also have an impact on the cost of your retirement. Consider what a dozen eggs cost just 10 years ago, versus what they cost now. Inflation affects every aspect of your financial life.

Here are some rough estimates to help you estimate how much you will need in retirement:

You'll need **65%** of your pre-retirement income if you:

o   Save a large amount (15% or more) of your annual earnings
o   Are a high-income earner
o   Will own your home free of debt by retirement
o   Plan to continue your current lifestyle choices

You'll need **75%** of your pre-retirement income if you:

o   Save a reasonable amount (5-14%) of your annual earnings
o   Will still have some mortgage debt in retirement
o   Anticipate a compatible standard to today in retirement

You'll need **85%** of your pre-retirement income if you:

- o   Save little or none of your annual earnings
- o   Will have a significant mortgage debt in retirement
- o   Want to maintain your current lifestyle in retirement

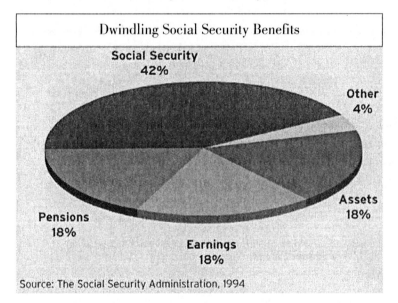

The most obvious source of retirement funds may be Social Security. But you cannot depend on Social Security to cover all of your financial needs in retirement. Today, Social Security benefits provide far less than the amount most people need, and may offer future generations much less. The relative number of Social Security contributors is shrinking. In 1945, 42 workers supported each retiree. However, in 2000, that number shrank to 3 workers supporting each retiree. By 2030, it's estimated that there may be only two workers for every retired person[1]. Longer life expectancies and the ever-increasing cost of living have had a profound effect on our Social Security system.

In the past, estimating your Social Security benefits was a difficult task, but not any longer. The Social Security Administration now provides an estimate of all future Social Security benefits to any taxpayer who requests it. The Social

Security Administration also sends yearly statements to all Americans aged 25 and older who have worked but are not yet receiving benefits. These statements are sent about three months before your birthday.

Both men and women should investigate the possibility of opening or adding to a qualified retirement account. Within certain limits, your annual contribution will be excluded from your current income for tax purposes. Your contribution plus the earnings on the contribution are not taxed until they are withdrawn. So be sure you are taking advantage of all employer-sponsored plans.

The best retirement strategy is to accumulate savings on your own—savings over which you have complete control. Tax-deferred growth can be an important part of this strategy. Individual retirement accounts (IRAs)—which are available to you whether you work as an employee or for yourself—can be advantageous because they provide tax-deferred growth, even if your contributions are not always tax deductible.

The Roth IRA offers tax-free accumulation and withdrawals. Although contributions to this type of IRA are not deductible, qualified distributions are not included in gross income or subject to the 10% penalty tax for early withdrawals (if distributed after a five-year holding period). Other exceptions also apply. Eligibility to make contributions phases out at higher modified adjusted gross income levels.

Even though IRAs offer ways to build and control retirement savings on a tax-deferred basis, each has a contribution limit and requires earned income. Many people—even those who are not working outside the home—may have a need to set aside an even greater amount of money for retirement outside of these plans.

Annuities supplement employer-sponsored retirement plans. They offer tax deferral and are not subject to the contribution limits of retirement plans. Your annuity can accumulate at a guaranteed fixed or variable rate, depending on the type of annuity you have purchased[16]. Earnings within an annuity also grow tax deferred until they are withdrawn. Your annuity can

---

[16]   Guarantee is based on the claims-paying ability of the insurer.

provide monthly payments to you at retirement that will continue for the rest of your life or for a specific term. Or, if you prefer, you can surrender your annuity contract and receive a lump sum when you retire.

To maximize your standard of living during retirement, you may need income from other personal savings and investments. You can choose from a variety of investment options such as stocks, bonds, and mutual funds. One main consideration when choosing investments for retirement is your time horizon. Early in your career, consider investments that offer potentially higher rates of return, keeping in mind the accompanying risk. Consider shifting to the lower risk/lower return vehicles as you get closer to retirement. You will also want to consider keeping some of your investments in growth vehicles while you are in retirement to help keep pace with inflation.

Retirement Plan Distributions

Before you receive a retirement plan distribution, do some planning in advance. Your decisions could affect your finances for the rest of your life. Generally speaking, you have two main choices: a lump sum or a rollover.

Lump Sum Distribution

If you take a lump sum distribution, you will pay income taxes. You can then spend or invest the balance as you wish. If you receive a cash distribution, 20% will be withheld for income taxes. That means you'll only really receive 80% of your distribution. Without proper planning, your distribution will be taxed at your marginal tax rate. However, planning may enable you to take advantage of special tax rules for lump sum distributions. For example, you may be able to take advantage of 10-year averaging, special capital gains treatment, or a combination of these rules, which may be able to save you a great deal in taxes. See your tax advisor for applicability of your unique circumstances.

Direct Rollover

To avoid the 20% withholding and continue the tax-deferred growth of your retirement plan, consider a direct rollover of your distribution to a self-directed IRA. With this method, you would arrange to have all of your money transferred from the trustee of the retirement plan to the custodian of your new IRA account. If you elect the IRA rollover, you won't be able to use the special tax rules for lump sum distributions. The rollover strategy may be beneficial when you want to continue tax-deferred growth for several more years, or start withdrawing a monthly check to supplement your income.

Annuity

If you elect an annuity, you will be taxed only on the income you receive each year. In many cases, you can receive payments over a set term, over your lifetime, or even over the life of you and your beneficiary. Many retirees choose an annuity because they are guaranteed an income and have several investment options available to them. Because the amount of each payment is fixed, you will also need to consider the effects of inflation on your income during your golden years.

With so many options available to help you prepare for retirement, it is still a typical human condition to postpone and procrastinate. Please, we urge you to take action. Imaging your retirement serves two critical purposes. First, it helps you put realistic numbers together to help you figure out how much in retirement assets you'll need. Second, and even more importantly, you are starting to visualize your own personal retirement dreams.

Years Spent In Retirement	
1900	1.2 years
1970	13.6 years
1990	19.4 years
2002	20-25 years

* By the year 2030, there will be 70 million people aged 65 and older, more than twice the population for that age group in 2000. Source: U.S. Bureau of Labor Statistics

Now is the operative word! The earlier you start saving for retirement, or any financial goal, the better. Year after year the money you invest can earn interest, dividends, and capital gains. If you reinvest those earnings in a tax-qualified retirement account, they'll generate additional earnings—a process known as tax-deferred compounding.

The more years spent planning and preparing for retirement, the higher the level of satisfaction!

Example:

Martha began saving $3,000 each year for retirement, starting with her first job when she was 25. Then, when Martha was 35 she stopped working to stay at home and care for her two newborn twin girls. Steve began saving for retirement at age 35 and continued to invest $3,000 every year for the next 30 years. The tax-deferred accounts of both investors earned 8% annually. Even though Steve contributed three times more than Martha, at age 65 her account was worth 62% more. Martha enjoyed the pleasure of having her initial savings of $30,000 grow to $535,434. By putting off starting a retirement savings account by just 10 years made a huge difference for Steve, whose account only grew to $331,462.

The amount of money you will need in future years depends on the lifestyle you plan to lead. Use your imagination to construct a picture of the way you want to live. Consider the following questions and the financial impact of each as you try to imagine

your retirement. If you are married, you and your spouse should
answer them together.

1. Do you plan on retiring? If so, when do you plan to stop
    working?
2. How would you describe the type of retirement lifestyle
    you'd like to live? Describe how you would like to spend
    your days.
3. Do you think you might like to keep working to stay
    active, or do you think you will need to work for financial
    concerns?
4. Do you have a desire to move?
5. How is your health?
6. What specific medical risks are you concerned about
    facing?
7. Do you have long-term care?
8. Do you think that you might have to care for a parent or
    in-law?
9. Do you plan to leave an inheritance to a child or
    grandchild?
10. What do you think you will want to do with your free
    time?
11. What are you doing to emotionally and financially prepare
    for your desired retirement?
12. What steps haven't you taken?
13. What questions do you have that need to be addressed?

📁 From The Real Life Files of Pat Vitucci
*The following is a real life example where the names have been
changed. But the situation described is accurate.*

Mario and Kathleen are 45 years old and they are empty
nesters. Their twin daughters recently graduated from college,
and have accepted new career positions in a neighbor city where

they will share an apartment. Mario and Kathleen's major
obligations for tuition and other educational expenses are
completed. Now they can focus on retirement planning.
Fortunately, both have participated in their respective 401(k)
plans at work but had to limit their contributions due to college
funding expenditures for their daughters. They now will enjoy a
significant increase in their monthly cash flow. Mario and Kathleen
are concerned about their priorities for investing.

Pat's Recommendation:

The priorities for investing are primarily centered on taxability.
Decisions to invest in pre-tax investments are priority number
one. Therefore, a maximum contribution in their respective 401(k)
plans is unquestionably the place to start. This will reduce their
taxable income and concurrently allow maximum tax deferred
growth.

Next, excess monthly cash available should be used to fund
Roth IRAs if your total income permits, based on IRS tax tables.
Refer to your tax consultant for income maximum eligibility.

Finally, monthly systematic electronic deductions from your
checking account should be swept into a collection of tax efficient
investments or a tax deferred account. Mario and Kathleen
certainly don't need more taxable income via dividends and/or
capital gains reports, so tax efficiency for post tax contributions
are essential.

A consultation with a financial advisor could provide a
projected savings and growth portfolio for the next 5, 10, 15, and
20 years, given a certain growth rate, inflation rate, and saving
amounts. These projections, while not definitive, will provide a
basic overview of what retirement life might resemble. Without
even a vague projection of your retirement goals being envisioned,
cash flow tends to be squandered on frivolous expensive
distractions. Life with moderation and balance, even in our
financial life, is important.

Key Points from Chapter 10:

1. Incorporate both a financial plan and healthy lifestyle choices to enjoy a very long life.
2. Regularly save and invest to gain financial independence.
3. Maximize tax-protected savings programs in your financial plans.

11

Financing a Child's Education

*Do not be fooled into believing that because a man is rich he
is necessarily smart. There is ample proof to the contrary.*
—Harry S Truman

Most people go to great lengths to take care of their
children, to make sure that they're happy. We get up at
dawn to drive them to hockey practice or stand in the drizzle to watch
a soccer match. We make sure they have music lessons, swimming
lessons, and tennis lessons. We shepherd them off to SAT tutoring
and meet with college counselors. We do all of this in hopes that our
children will have successful, productive lives. We're sure you've seen
the bumper stickers: My kid and my money go to _____
University! It doesn't have to be entirely tongue in cheek.

Please be conscious that we want you to be sure you provide
for your own financial security before saving for your child. Just
like on the airplane, in the event of a loss of air pressure that

necessitates the use of oxygen masks, you are instructed to put YOUR oxygen mask on FIRST. Only then should you help your children with their oxygen masks. Consider for a moment why airlines recommend this approach. Although your instinct may be to ensure that your children are safe before taking care of yourself, by taking care of yourself first, you are stronger and better able to help your children.

A child's college education may be the single largest expense some parents will face. How much does a college education cost today? For the 2000-2001 school year, the average total cost for one year at a four-year private college was $27,711. For four-year public institutions, the average price tag was $9,326. These numbers are rather large, but don't let them overwhelm you. The following three-step plan can help you reach this long-term goal.

First, estimate how much your child's college education may cost. If college costs continue to increase at nearly double the rate of inflation—as they did during the 1990s—the average total cost of a four-year private university will soar to $321,273 by the time a child born in 2001 enters college in 2019. The average annual increase in college costs may turn out to be higher or lower than projected here, and you may choose a school that is more or less expensive than average. These estimates are only intended to provide you a useful starting point for developing your financial plan.

Second, build your investment one month at a time. No matter how much you need to save, the most important step is to BEGIN investing. Third, don't ignore the high cost of procrastinating. Suppose your child is scheduled to enter college in 10 years— when four years at a public university may cost you about $70,927. You can either begin making regular investments today, or wait until 2011 and finance the costs. You could save more than $45,000 by beginning a regular investment program now, rather than borrowing that amount later. Once again, you'll be able to take advantage of our sweet friend "compound interest."

The third step is to sidestep taxes (legally, of course). Income taxes can take a big bite out of your investment earnings, so it pays to investigate options that may help you limit, or even avoid, some taxes.

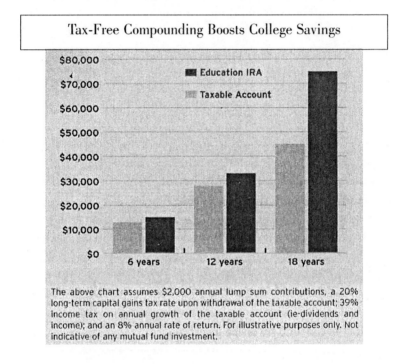

Tax-Free Compounding Boosts College Savings

The above chart assumes $2,000 annual lump sum contributions, a 20% long-term capital gains tax rate upon withdrawal of the taxable account; 39% income tax on annual growth of the taxable account (ie-dividends and income); and an 8% annual rate of return. For illustrative purposes only. Not indicative of any mutual fund investment.

529 College Plans

A 529 college plan is a qualified tuition program under Section 529 of the Internal Revenue Code. Such plans are state administered, but states often utilize mutual fund companies to provide underlying investment vehicles and related services to the plan. It offers families an effective college investment tool with various benefits, including:

- Tax free growth for all income levels. Contributions are not deductible, but for qualified distributions, earnings are distributed free of federal taxes until December 31, 2010 (this may change if the tax laws are extended beyond this date.)

- High contribution limits. Each plan sets its own limits, often $175,000 or more per child—allowing the potential for rapid asset buildup.

- Special gift and estate tax treatment. Annual contributions are generally excluded for federal gift and estate tax purposes, up to $11,000 per beneficiary ($22,000 for married couples filing jointly). In addition, provided additional gifts are not made to the same beneficiary over the next five years, no gift tax will result if a contributor elects on a federal gift tax return to contribute up to $55,000 ($110,000 for married couples filing jointly) to each beneficiary in the first year of a five-year period.

- Professionally managed portfolios such as age progression portfolios and fixed asset allocations can help with your college planning.

UGMAs / UTMAs

If you invest in your own name, earnings are taxed based on your marginal income tax rate. One way you may save on taxes is to place assets in your child's name through an UGMA (Uniform Gifts to Minors Act) or UTMA (Uniform Transfers to Minors Act) account.

The Internal Revenue Code allows children under the age of 14 to receive $750 of unearned income per year, such as interest or dividends, on a tax-free basis. The next $750 of unearned income is taxed at the child's rate, and any unearned income over $1,500 is taxed at the higher of the child's or the parent's marginal rate. After the age of 14, all income is taxed at the child's rate. However, gifts and transfers to minors are irrevocable and give complete control of the money to the child at majority (age 18 or 21, depending on the state).

Coverdell Education Savings Accounts

Many individuals may contribute $2,000 per year, per child (under age of 18 or designated as a Special Needs Beneficiary), to a Coverdell Education Savings Account. The investment is not deductible, but the income it earns is tax free upon withdrawal, as long as it is used to pay for qualifying education costs such as tuition and certain room and board expenses.

Now that we've briefly outlined some of the basic educational investments, you need to now determine which investment could put your savings objective within reach. Your child's age determines your investment time frame and is an important factor in determining your risk tolerance level. Stocks have historically generated higher, long-term returns than bonds or Treasury bills but have also had greater volatility, meaning your assets could lose value when you need them most. You may want to choose investments with the greatest potential returns when your child is young, but reduce the risk exposure as your child nears college age.

A Special Note to Grandparents:

Grandparents (and other financially secure relatives) can pass assets to children without giving cash—and without setting off the $10,000 limit. There are several avenues you can explore and utilize for your young family members to get a first-rate education.

- First, name your grandchild as a beneficiary. If you're worried that you won't be around to help a young grandchild with college or other expenses, you can name that child a beneficiary of a life insurance policy. If your concern is putting too much money in the child's hands too soon (and you probably should be), stipulate in your will that the payout be recorded in a trust. Then name a trustee who will make sure that the payout is used for tuition.

- Set up an intergenerational transfer trust. Besides allowing you to leave $1 million to your heirs without incurring estate taxes, the government lets you leave an additional $1 million (in total) to grandkids with no tax. It's called generation skipping, and everyone is entitled to take advantage.

- Pay tuition or medical bills outright. You can ignore gift taxes entirely if you pay medical bills or tuition for your grandchildren. The wrinkle is that these payments must go directly to the college, private school, hospital or doctor to whom they are owed. The rule applies only to tuition, not to room and board, but you could give your grandchild a $10,000 gift to cover those expenses.

- Make a lump sum contribution to a college plan. As we discussed before, state-sponsored college savings plans (such as 529 plans) allow contributions of up to $55,000 in one year, as long as you don't make subsequent 529 deposits for that child for the four years following. The IRS will look at this as if you've made five consecutive $11,000 annual gifts. Note: if the grandchild for whom you contributed the money decides not to go to college, the funds are completely portable to other children, or for you or your spouse's educational costs.

- Pay off student loans. If you're concerned that giving to your grandchild will hamper their ability to qualify for financial aid, you may want to make a gift after graduation. Then, using the annual $11,000 gifts, you can help them pay off their student loans.

- Give stocks to your grandkids. If you own a stock more than a year and you sell, you'd likely be taxed at the 20% rate. If you give the stock to your grandkids over the age of 14 who are in the 15% tax bracket when they sell the stock, they'll pay only 10% in capital gains. And if your grandkids hold the stock for at least five years in total, the tax on the capital gains could drop to as little as 8%. Please consult with your tax professional for a complete picture of all the tax implications.

Many well-intentioned parents want to save for their children's future educational expenses. The mistake they often make, however, is putting money in accounts with their child's name or saving outside of retirement type accounts in general. Why would this be a problem? First, you receive no tax deduction on your contributions to these accounts. However, your retirement account contributions are not only tax-deductible in the year made but also grow compound tax-deferred. The second problem with under-funding retirement accounts is that the more money you accumulate outside tax-sheltered retirement accounts, the less assistance you're likely to qualify for from federal and state financial aid sources.

Under the current financial needs analysis that most colleges use in awarding financial aid, the value of your retirement plan is not considered an asset. Money that you save outside retirement accounts, including money in the child's name, is counted as an asset and can reduce your eligibility for financial aid.

If you plan to apply for financial aid, it's a good idea to save non-retirement account money in your name rather than in your child's names. Colleges expect a greater percentage of money in your child's name (35%) to be used for college costs than money in your name (6%). Also be aware that your family's assets, for purposes of financial aid determination, also include equity in real estate and businesses you own. Although the federal financial aid analysis no longer counts equity in your primary residence as an asset, many private (independent) schools continue to ask parents for this information when making their own financial aid determinations. Again, paying down your home mortgage more quickly instead of funding retirement accounts can harm you financially. You may end up with less financial aid and pay more in taxes.

If you keep up to 80% of your investment money in diversified mutual funds with the remainder in bonds when your child is young, you should maximize the money's growth potential without taking extraordinary risk. As your child is making his or her way through the later years of elementary school, begin to make the mix more conservative. Finally during your child's final high school years, you should have the stock portion whittled down to a very small percentage.

Your financial advisor can help you determine which funds are best suited for your college investment plan, based on your investment time frame and the degree of risk you find acceptable.

An additional note: Sadly, many Americans don't know how to manage their personal finances because in most cases, they were never taught how to do so. Nearly all our high schools and colleges lack even one course to teach this vital, lifelong-needed skill. Fortunate and lucky people learn the financial keys to success at home or from knowledgeable friends. Others never learn or learn the hard way: by making lots of costly mistakes. Lack of proficiency in personal financial management causes not only tremendous anxiety, but can also lead to some serious problems. In some families, financial illiteracy is passed on from generation to generation.

We'd like to encourage you to actively engage your child or grandchild in the financial challenges necessary to fund their education. Using these investments as tools to make the younger members of your family aware and educated could be one of the most valuable lessons you can offer them. The overall costs of personal financial illiteracy to our society are huge. The high rate of spending and low rate of saving in the United States leads to lower long-term economic growth and higher interest rates.

In many families money is a taboo subject—parents don't level with their kids about the limitations, realities, and details of their budgets. Some parents we talk with believe that dealing with money is an adult only issue. Don't underestimate our youth's potential or send them out into the world without the skills they need to be productive and happy adults. Talk to them and have them join you when you meet with your financial advisor.

📁 From The Real Life Files of Pat Vitucci
The following is a real life example where the names have been changed. But the situation described is accurate.

Ron and Donna are the proud grandparents of four children, two boys—ages 3 and 5, and two girls—ages 7 and 9. The parents of these grandchildren have been unable to save any money given their very tight budgets. Ron and Donna are recently retired and are capable of beginning to fund college savings plans for their grandchildren. They are concerned about the control of these monies given the fact that their children have not exercised sound financial discipline and, consequently, may be tempted to cash out these funds to continue to support their "high lifestyles."

Pat's Recommendation:

Grandma and Grandpa should open four 529 College Savings Plans, naming themselves as the custodian, thereby, retaining complete control over the funds. Their estate plans (wills and trusts) should name successor trustees to manage these dollars. Rather than buying more toys at birthdays, holidays, or other occasions, continue to make deposits into all four accounts. Ron and Donna can elect to transfer any child's account to the others, should that child decide that college is not for him or her. These are not monies for that hot, new convertible car; these dollars are completely portable without the consequences to be used for college expenses.

Key Points from Chapter 11:

1. One of the best educational plans you can give your child is to teach them the importance of saving and investing.
2. Utilize tax-free compounding when saving for college.
3. Talk to a financial advisor to determine which college saving plan is right for your situation.

12

Financial Spirituality

Make money your god and it will plague you like the devil.—
Henry Fielding

The world of money, of numbers and stock markets and interest rates and credit cards, seems on the surface about as far as it could be from the world of spirituality, of seeking meaningful answers to the big questions in life. Everyone has the same amount of time, yet not everyone has the same amount of money. Money represents a summation of your life, your work and your time in a tangible form. Yet, why are there contrasting amounts among people?

As Jacob Needleman writes in his book, *Money and the Meaning of Life,* "Our challenge is to bring money back to the place where it belongs in human life. It is not a question of getting more money, although for you or me that may be necessary. It is not a question of giving up money, although, again, for you or me that may be necessary up to a point. It is not even a question of ordering one's life—tidying up one's affairs, necessary though that may be for you or me sometimes. It is solely a question of restoring money to its proper place in human life. And that place is secondary." (p. 70)

Proverbs 21:20 states, "In the house of the wise are stores of choice feed and oil, but a foolish man devours all he has." One of the keys to financial stewardship is to bring our will into line with God's will. Begin by listening with your hearts and minds to make sound, logical reflective decisions. Then, shift your perspective to think long term.

The founder of the Methodist church, John Wesley, stated these three stewardship principles over 200 years ago and they are still pertinent today:

1. Work all you can.
2. Save all you can.
3. Give all you can.

Let's take a look at how we can apply each of these to our lives in today's world. God has given each a job to accomplish while we are here on Earth. Granted, some days it isn't too clear, or it's not always the job we would wish for ourselves. But that shouldn't distract us from our purpose. As stated in I Timothy 5:8, "If anyone does not provide for his relatives, and especially for his immediate family, he has denied the faith and is worse than an unbeliever." We are truly commanded by God to work and provide for our families. As Dr. Martin Luther King, Jr. once pointed out during a speech, "Whatever you do—be it a street sweeper or teacher—do it with all your heart, all your might, and do the best job you can with the talents that God has given you."

With the overload of "buy now" and "great deals" continually bombarding us by the media, it is very easy to be lured into thinking that without purchasing the latest gadget our lives will be torture. We should consider re-thinking this lifestyle. Another problem that usually accompanies those selling messages is one of "buy on time." In moderation, credit can be an ally, but when used indiscriminately it can be a severe adversary to good stewardship. The truth is to think long term. If we can step out of society's flashpoint lifestyle to see the bigger picture, we are in a better mindset to not only understand money, but also to understand God's will for us. Saving is like any other habit, hard to stick to at first—but once you're over that hurdle it becomes a natural part of your life. This is where we can take advantage of many conveniences—such as automatic deductions at work into a 401(k) account and savings accounts. When you start telling yourself you can't save, think back to a time in your life when you were able to get by each month with a smaller paycheck. It is often that greed can sometimes be a culprit for our lack of saving. One popular financial advisor has pointed out that many people with over-flowing closets, cabinets, and garages usually also have an over-flowing credit card and an empty savings account. Starting today, begin to ask yourself each time you pick up an item at the store, "Do I really need this?" We think you'll be amazed how often the real answer is an overwhelming no. But before you head out to the store, start going through those closets, cabinets, and full garages—chances are you already have whatever you need right there in your home.

Another perspective to keep in mind is to look within and determine what you are truly honoring by the debts you've created with your spending habits. Some people spend a tremendous amount of money on their hobby or kitchen gadgets or car tools. Yet, fail to save for the emergencies that are bound to happen in everyone's life. Where is their focus? Is this the lifestyle pattern God has outlined for us? In Romans 3:18 we are reminded, "Let no debt remain outstanding, expect the continuing debt to love one another, for he who loves his fellow man has fulfilled the law."

In our hectic, busy lives it is easy to loose sight of principle number two. But to save is also commanded to us in the Bible. In Malachi 3:8-10 it is written, "Will a man rob God? Yet you rob me. But you ask, 'How do we rob you?' In tithes and offerings. You are under a curse—the whole nation of you—because you are robbing me. Bring the whole tithe into the storehouse, that there may be food in my house. Test me in this," says the Lord Almighty, "and see if I will not throw open the floodgates of heaven and pour out so much blessing that you will not have room enough for it." See, God wants to bless us with an over abundance—if we will just offer Him our tithes.

A good rule of thumb for the Christian household budget is the 10/10/80 rule. The first 10 percent of your money is given back to God. He is to be given the first fruits of our labors. It is through God's grace that we live and it is a privilege to honor Him with our gifts. The second 10 percent of your money is to be saved. God wants us to enjoy a happy, full life. He truly does not want His children to live with worry and fear. One of the best ways to eliminate worry and fear from your life is to have a savings account to cushion you when the "accidents" and "emergencies" happen, as they do in every one's life. The final 80 percent is what you should use to pay for your living expenses. It is not only important to realize that you should be living on less than 100% (or even 110%) of your income, but the order of whom you should pay. God is first, and then your savings, with everyone and everything else last. We are definitely not suggesting you not pay your bills or be delinquent with your payments. We are suggesting that you carefully and prayerfully reconsider your stewardship if the 10/10/80 plan isn't one that you are currently following. Like all financial habits, it can easily be a goal you work towards. But, begin today to shape your budget towards this simple outline. The rewards are amazing and worth the small sacrifice.

Please imagine that you've gone into your kitchen and turned on the faucet. Make a tight fist with both your hands and try to get a filling drink of water. You won't be able to will you? Now open up your hands and form a cup. Put them under the water and they will soon be overflowing. Your thirst will soon be quenched. It can work the same with our money. If we are grasping what we have so tightly, we are not open to receive or even take advantage of all that is flowing our way. We must learn to open our grasp and trust that God will provide.

With our clients we've found an interesting theory. We divided them into two groups: one that gives money to a charity (or church) on a regular basis, and those that don't. What we found was that those that gave often seemed to have an abundance of money, and the others didn't. We're not suggesting that people who don't regularly give to charities aren't able to live abundant, rich lives. But we are suggesting that we've seen the results of those who make it a part of their financial lives to share with others. These folks are not only more content in their own lives, but are contributing to helping others. This more than the money they give is what God is commanding us to do.

In the Eastern spiritual tradition, there is the dharma of money, which means the "right action" of money. It follows a principle: we will experience prosperity, true financial freedom, when our actions with respect to money are dharmic, or righteous, actions— that is, actions of generosity, actions of offerings. Money flows through our lives just like water—at times plentiful, at times only a small trickle.

You open yourself to receive all that is meant to be yours. Giving not only when you feel poor, but also when you feel rich, lucky, grateful, expansive, and vital. Giving to say please and giving to say thank you. It's the impulse to give that puts you in touch with the best part of yourself—and the principles of abundance that are alive in the world.

Regardless of how much money you have, it is the natural tendency of the mind to think: I can't give money this month; I don't even have enough to pay the bills. Or, there are so many things that I need, I lack, I want. We challenge you to rethink that thinking. This is the exact moment to give, to give an amount that is meaningful but realistic. You must break these thoughts of poverty, for thoughts of poverty are chains that keep you bound to poverty. Mental chains may be invisible but they imprison you nonetheless. You must and you can break through, to move beyond these barriers. You cup your hands to receive more. Remind yourself of how much you have, think about those with far less, and give thanks with your gift.

True financial freedom is a powerful state of mind and one that God wants us to achieve. It is a state of being that comes from following his commandments and guidelines for stewardship. With your offerings you are participating in the flow of wealth, which with God's generosity, is never-ending. It isn't how much you have that creates a sense of freedom. It's how you feel about what you have, and don't have, that either keeps you a prisoner or sets you free.

Let's see things from God's perspective:

- Look beyond tomorrow—plan and manage your talents for the best return on them in the future.
- God is not anti-money, or anti-wealth. He is anti-money worship.
- Learn to be content in every situation.

"Whatsoever a man sows that will he also reap" proclaims Galatians 6:7. The stewardship of our money is entirely up to us, and it is another opportunity that God gives us to demonstrate our love to Him. With that in mind, we need to be especially careful in making solid, educated investment choices. We need to think long term and diversify our money. Finally, we need to live a balanced life with everything in moderation. Decisions, particularly regarding our financial life, should be thoughtful and reflective of our purpose to serve and honor God.

Imagine how it feels to be on a noisy trading floor on Wall Street. Imagine instead how it feels to be alone in a quiet peaceful place of worship. But these two worlds must flow together, because it takes both money and spiritual understanding to sustain us. If we quietly listen within ourselves, the answers about how we should use our money will be revealed to us.

We have learned what a truly powerful force money can be, how it can create fears, how it can paralyze us, and how it can provide us with freedom. We have learned about the dharma of money, the essential right actions that, once taken, will put our money and us in step with the life we desire. Most important, we have learned an essential lesson of abundance.

Once we have taken care of the people we love, it is worthy to accumulate money. With the responsibility of accumulating money, however, comes the equally urgent responsibility of using money wisely. The rich man who takes no pleasure in his wealth and does not share will not enjoy the true pleasures of money and be free. People with a much more modest income, but a love to serve God in their heart and actions, will in the end enjoy a far richer reward.

Key Points from Chapter 12:

1. Utilize the 10/10/80 financial plan towards supporting your church or charity organization.
2. Track where your money is being spent to see if it is in alignment with your values.
3. Open yourself to receive all you can, by giving all you can.

Glossary of Terms

My problem lies in reconciling my gross habits
with my net income.—Errol Flynn

Adjusted Gross Income (AGI)—An interim calculation in the computation of income tax liability. It is computed by subtracting certain allowable adjustments from gross income.

Administrator—A person appointed by the court to settle an estate when there is no will.

After-Tax Return—The return from an investment after the effects of taxes have been taken into account.

Aggressive Growth Fund—A mutual fund whose primary investment objective is substantial capital gains.

Alternative Minimum Tax—A method of calculating income tax that disallows certain deductions, credits, and exclusions. This was intended to ensure that individuals, trusts, and estates that benefit from tax preferences do not escape all federal income tax liability. People must calculate their taxes both ways and pay the greater of the two.

Annuity—An insurance-based contract that provides future payments at regular intervals in exchange for current premiums. Annuity contracts are usually purchased from banks, credit unions, brokerage firms, or insurance companies.

Asset Allocation—The process of repositioning assets within a portfolio to maximize the return for a given level of risk. This process is usually done using the historical performance of the asset classes within sophisticated mathematical methods.

Asset Class—A category of investments with similar characteristics.

Audit—The examination of the accounting and financial documents of a firm by an objective professional. The audit is done to determine the record's accuracy, consistency, and conformity to legal and accounting principles.

Balanced Mutual Fund—A mutual fund whose objective is purchasing a balance of stocks and bonds. Such funds tend to be less volatile than stock-only funds.

Beneficiary—A person named in a life insurance policy, annuity, will, trust, or other agreement to receive a financial benefit upon the death of the owner. A beneficiary can be an individual, company, organization, and so on.

Blue Chip—The common stock of a company with a long history of profitability and consistent dividend payment.

Bond—A bond is simply an I.O.U. by a corporation that promises to pay the holder of the piece of paper a fixed sum of money at the specified maturity date and some other fixed amount of money (the coupon or the interest payment) every year up to the date of maturity.

Book Values—The net value of a company's assets, less its liabilities and the liquidation price of its preferred issues. The net assets value divided by the number of shares of common stock outstanding equals the book value per share, which may be higher or lower than the stock's market value.

Capital Gain—The difference between the price at which an asset is sold and the price at which it was bought.

Cash Equivalents—Short-term investments, such as U.S. Treasury securities, certificates of deposit, and money market fund shares, which can be readily converted into cash.

Cash Surrender Value—The amount that an insurance policyholder is entitled to receive when he or she discontinues coverage. Policyholders are usually able to borrow against the surrender value of a policy from the insurance company.

Certificate of Deposit (CD)—A savings certificate entitling the bearer to receive interest. A CD bears a maturity date, a specified interest rate, and can be issued in any denomination. CDs are generally issued by commercial banks.

Charitable Lead Trust—A trust established for the benefit of a charitable organization under which the charitable organization receives income from an asset for a set number of years of for the trustor's lifetime. Upon the termination of the trust, the asset reverts to the trustor or to his or her designated heirs. This type of trust reduces estate taxes and allows the heirs to retain control of the assets.

Charitable Remainder Trust—A trust established for the benefit of a charitable organization under which the trustor receives income from an asset for a set number of years or for the trustor's lifetime. Upon the termination of the trust, the asset reverts to the charitable organization. The trustor receives a charitable contribution deduction in the year in which the trust is established and is exempted from capital gains tax on the assets placed in the trust.

Common Stock—A common stock of a corporation is a piece of paper that gives the holder of the stock a share of the ownership of the company.

Community Property—State laws vary, but generally, all property acquired during a marriage—excluding property one spouse receives from a will, inheritance, or gift—is considered community property, and each partner is entitled to one half. This includes debt accumulated. There are currently nine community property states: Arizona, California, Idaho, Louisiana, Nevada, New Mexico, Texas, Washington, and Wisconsin.

Compound Interest—Interest that is computed on the principal and on the accrued interest. Compound interest may be computed continuously, daily, monthly, quarterly, semiannually, or annually.

Corporation—A corporation is a firm that has the legal status of a fictional individual. This fictional individual is owned by a number of persons, called its stockholders, and is run by a set of elected officers and a board of directors, whose chairman is often also in a powerful position.

Deduction—An amount that can be subtracted from gross income, from a gross estate, or from a gift, thereby lowering the amount on which tax is assessed.

Defined Benefit Plan—A qualified retirement plan under which a retiring employee will receive a guaranteed retirement fund usually payable in installments. Annual contributions may be made to the plan by the employer at the level needed to fund the benefit. The annual contributions are limited to a specified amount, indexed to inflation.

Defined Contribution Plan—A qualified retirement plan under which the annual contributions made by the employer or employee are generally stated as a fixed percentage of the employee's compensation or company profits. The amount of retirement benefits is not guaranteed; rather, it depends upon the investment performance of the employee's account.

Deflation—Deflation refers to a sustained decrease in the general price level.

Devaluation—Devaluation is a reduction in the official value of a currency.

Discount Rate—The discount rate is the interest rate the Federal Reserve Board charges on loans that it makes to banks.

Diversification—Investing in different companies, industries, or asset classes. Diversification may also mean the participation of a large corporation in a wide range of business activities.

Dividend—A pro rata portion of earnings distributed in cash by a corporation to its stockholders. In preferred stock, dividends are usually fixed; with common shares, dividends may vary with the fortunes of the company.

Dollar Cost Averaging—A system of investing in which the investor buys a fixed dollar amount of securities at regular intervals. The investor thus buys more shares when the price is low and fewer shares when it rises, and the average cost per share is lower than the average price per share.

Employer-Sponsored Retirement Plan—A tax-favored retirement plan that is sponsored by an employer. Among the more common employer-sponsored retirement plans are 401(k) plans, 403(b) plans, simplified employee pension plans, and profit sharing plans.

Equity—The value of a person's ownership in real property or securities; the market value of a property or business, less all claims and liens upon it.

ERISA—The Employee Retirement Income Security Act is a federal law covering all aspects of employee retirement plans. If employers provide plans, they must be adequately funded and provide for vesting, survivor's rights, and disclosures.

ESOP (employee stock ownership plan)—A defined contribution retirement plan in which company contributions must be invested primarily in qualifying employer securities.

Estate Planning—Activities coordinated to provide for the orderly and cost-effective distribution of an individual's assets at the time of his or her death. Estate planning often includes wills and trusts.

Estate Tax—Upon the death of a decedent, federal and state governments impose taxes on the value of the estate left to others (with limitations).

Exchange Rate—The exchange rate states the price, in terms of one currency, at which another currency can be bought.

Executor—A person named by the probate courts or the will to carry out the directions and requests of the decedent.

Fiscal Policy—The government's fiscal policy is its plan for spending and taxation. It is designed to steer aggregate demand in some desired direction.

Fixed Income—Income from investments such as CDs, Social Security benefits, pension benefits, some annuities, or most bonds that is the same every month.

401(k) Plan—A defined contribution plan that may be established by a company for retirement. Employees may allocate a portion of their salaries into this plan, and contributions are excluded from their income for tax purposes (with limitations). Earnings will compound tax deferred.

403(b) Plan—A defined contribution plan that may be established by a non-profit organization or school for retirement. Employees may allocate a portion of their salaries into this plan, and contributions are excluded from their income for tax purposes (with limitations). Earnings will compound tax deferred.

Gift Taxes—A federal tax levied on the transfer of property as a gift. This tax is paid by the donor. The first $10,000 a year from a donor to each recipient is exempt from tax. Most states also impose a gift tax.

Gross Domestic Product (GDP)—Gross Domestic Product (GDP) is a measure of the size of an economy. It is, roughly speaking, the money value of all the goods and services produced in a year.

Individual Retirement Account (IRA)—With a traditional IRA, annual contributions up to a defined amount are deductible from earned income in the calculation of federal and state income taxes if the taxpayer meets certain requirements. The earnings accumulate tax deferred until withdrawn, and then they are taxed as ordinary income. Individuals not eligible to make deductible contributions may make nondeductible contributions, the earnings on which would be tax deferred. Two new nondeductible IRAs are the Roth IRA and the Educational IRA.

Inflation—Inflation refers to a sustained increase in the average level of prices.

Interest—Interest is the payment for the use of funds employed in the production of capital; it is measured as a percentage per year of the value of the funds tied up in the capital.

Intestate—A person who dies without leaving a valid will. State law then determines who inherits the property or serves as the guardian for any minor children.

Joint and Survivor Annuity—Most pension plans must offer this form of pension plan payout that pays over the life of the retiree and his or her spouse after the retiree dies. The retiree and his or her spouse must specifically choose not to accept this payment form.

Jointly Held Property—Property owned by two or more persons under joint tenancy, tenancy in common, or in some states, community property.

Joint Tenancy—Co-ownership of property by two or more people in which the survivor(s) automatically assume ownership of a decedent's interest.

Keogh Plan—This is a type of retirement plan named for Eugene Keogh, and it is designed for self-employed individuals. Up to $35,000 or 25% of self-employed income (whichever is less) may be deducted from compensation and set aside into the plan.

Labor Productivity—Labor productivity refers to the amount of output a worker turns out in an hour (or a week or a year) of labor. It can be measured as total national output (GDP) in a given year divided by the total number of hours of work performed for pay in the country during that year. That is, labor productivity is defined as GDP per hour of labor.

Liability—A liability of an individual or business firm is an item of value that the individual or firm owes. Many liabilities are known as debts.

Limited Partnership—Limited partnerships pool the money of investors to develop or purchase income-producing properties. When the partnership subsequently receives income from these properties, it passes the income on to its investors as dividend payments.

Liquidity—The ease with which an asset or security can be converted into cash without loss of principal.

Lump Sum Distribution—The disbursement of the entire value of a profit sharing plan, pension plan, annuity, or similar account to the account owner or beneficiary. Lump sum distributions may be rolled over into another tax-deferred account.

Marginal Tax Bracket—The range of taxable income that is taxable at a certain rate.

Marital Deduction—A provision of the tax codes that allows all the assets of a deceased spouse to pass to the surviving spouse free from estate taxes. This provision is also referred to as the unlimited martial deduction.

Monetary Policy—Monetary policy refers to actions that the Federal Reserve System takes in order to change the equilibrium of the money market; that is, to alter the money supply, move interest rates, or both.

Money Market Fund—A mutual fund that specializes in investing in short-term securities and that tries to maintain a constant net asset value of $1.

Municipal Bond—A debt security issued by municipalities. The income from municipal bonds is usually exempt from federal income taxes. In many states, it is also exempt from state income taxes in the state in which the municipal bond is issued.

Municipal Bond Fund—A mutual fund that specializes in investing in municipal bonds.

Mutual Fund—A collection of stocks, bonds, or other securities purchased and managed by an investment company with funds from a group of investors.

National Debt—The national debt is the federal government's total indebtedness at a moment of time. It is the result of previous deficits.

National Income—National income is the sum of the incomes that all individuals in the economy earned in the forms of wages, interest, rents, and profits. It excludes transfer payments and is calculated before any deductions are taken for income taxes.

Net Asset Value—The price at which a mutual fund sells or redeems its shares. The net asset value is calculated by dividing the net market value of the fund's assets by the number of outstanding shares.

Net Worth—Net worth is the value of all assets minus the value of all liabilities.

Partnership—A partnership is a firm whose ownership is shared by a fixed number of proprietors.

Proprietorship—A proprietorship is a business firm owned by a single person.

Personal Financial Management Professional—A financial services professional that helps individuals coordinate their financial affairs to achieve their financial objectives.

Pooled Income Fund—A trust created by a charitable organization that combines the contributions of several donors and distributes income to those donors based on the earnings of the trust. The trust is managed by the charitable organization, and contributions are partially deductible for income tax purposes.

Preferred Stock—A class of stock with claim to a company's earnings before payment can be made on the common stock and usually entitled to priority over common stock if the company liquidates. Generally, preferred stocks pay dividends at a fixed rate.

Prenuptial Agreement—A legal agreement arranged before marriage stating who owns property acquired before marriage and during marriage and how property will be divided in the event of divorce. ERISA benefits are not affected by prenuptial agreements.

Price/Earnings Ratio (P/E Ratio)—The market price of a stock divided by the company's annual earnings per share. Since the P/E ratio is a widely regarded yardstick for investors, it often appears with stock price quotations.

Probate—The court-supervised process in which a decedent's estate is settled and distributed.

Profit Sharing Plan—An agreement under which employees share in the profits of their employer. The company makes annual contributions to the employee's account. These funds usually accumulate tax deferred until the employee retires or leaves the company.

Qualified Domestic Relations Order (QDRO)—At the time of a divorce, this order would be issues by a state domestic relations court and would require that an employee's ERISA retirement plan accrued benefits be divided between the employee and the spouse.

Qualified Retirement Plan—A pension, profit sharing, or qualified savings plan that is established by an employer for the benefit of the employees. These plans must be established in conformity with IRS rules. Contributions accumulate tax deferred until withdrawn and are deductible to the employer as a current business expense.

Real GDP—Real GDP is the value of all the goods and services produced by an economy in a year, evaluated in dollars of constant purchasing power. Hence, inflation does not raise real GDP.

Real Rate of Interest—The real rate of interest is the percentage increase in purchasing power that the borrower pays to the lender for the privilege of borrowing. It indicates the increased ability to purchase goods and services that the lender earns.

Real Wage Rate—The real wage rate is the wage rate adjusted for inflation. It indicates the volume of goods and services that money wages will buy.

Recession—A recession is a period of time during which the total output of the economy falls.

Risk-Averse—Refers to the assumption that rational investors will choose the security with the least risk if they can maintain the same return. As the level of risk goes up, so must the expected return on the investment.

Rollover—A method by which an individual can transfer the assets from one retirement program to another without the recognition of income for tax purposes. The requirements for a rollover depend on the type of program from which the distribution is made and the type of program receiving the distribution.

Roth IRA—A special type of IRA that offers tax-free accumulation and withdrawals if certain conditions are met. Contributions are nondeductible, and qualified distributions are not included in your gross income.

SEP (simplified employee pension plan)—A type of plan under which the employer contributes to an employee's IRA. Contributions may be made up to a certain limit and are immediately vested.

Single-Life Annuity—An insurance-based contract that provides future payments at regular intervals in exchange for current premiums. Generally used as a supplement to retirement income and pays over the life of one individual, usually the retiree, with no rights of payment to any survivor.

Spousal IRA—An IRA designed for a couple when one spouse has no earned income. The maximum contribution that can be made each year to an IRA and spousal IRA is $4,000 or 100% of earned income, whichever is less.

Stagflation—Stagflation is inflation that occurs while the economy is growing slowly ("stagnating") or having a recession.

Taxable Income—The amount of income used to compute tax liability. It is determined by subtracting adjustments, itemized deductions or the standard deduction, and personal exemptions from gross income.

Tax Credit—Tax credits are subtracted directly, dollar-for-dollar, from your income tax bill.

Tax Deferred—Interest, dividends, or capital gains that grow untaxed in certain accounts or plans until they are withdrawn.

Tax-Exempt Bonds—Under certain conditions, the interest from bonds issued by states, cities, and certain other government agencies is exempt from federal income taxes. In many states, the interest from tax-exempt bonds will also be exempt from state and local taxes.

Tenancy in Common—A form of co-ownership. Upon the death of a co-owner, his or her interest passes to his or her chosen beneficiaries and not to the surviving owner or owners.

Term Insurance—Term life insurance provides a death benefit if the insured dies. Term insurance does not accumulate cash value and ends after a certain number of years or at a certain age.

Testator—One who has made a will or dies leaving a will.

Total Return—The total of all earnings from a given investment including dividends, interest, and any capital gain.

Trust—A legal entity created by an individual in whom one person or institution holds the right to manage property or assets for the benefit of someone else. Types of trusts include:

> **Testamentary Trust**—A trust established by a will that takes effect upon death.

> **Living Trust**—A trust created by a person during his or her lifetime.

> **Revocable Trust**—A trust in which the creator reserves the right to modify or terminate the trust.

> **Irrevocable Trust**—A trust that may not be modified or terminated by the trustor after its creation.

Trustee—An individual or institution appointed to administer a trust for its beneficiaries.

Trustee-to-Trustee Transfer—A method of transferring retirement plan assets from one employer's plan to another employer's plan or to an IRA. One benefit of this method is that no federal income tax will be withheld by the trustee of the first plan.

Unemployment Rate—The unemployment rate is the number of unemployed people, expressed as a percentage of the labor force.

Unified Credit—A credit that may be applied against an individual's gift or estate tax.

Universal Life Insurance—A type of life insurance that combines a death benefit with a cash-value element that accumulates tax deferred at current interest rates. Under a universal life insurance policy, the policy holder can increase or decrease his or her coverage, with limitations, without purchasing a new policy.

Variable Universal Life Insurance—A type of life insurance that combines a death benefit with a cash-value element that accumulates tax deferred at current interest rates. Under a variable universal life insurance policy, the cash value in the policy can be invested in a variety of investment sub-accounts. The policyholder can transfer funds among the sub-accounts as he or she wishes.

Volatility—The range of price swings of a security or market over time.

Whole Life Insurance—A type of life insurance that offers a death benefit and also accumulates cash value, tax deferred at fixed interest rates. Whole life insurance policies generally have a fixed annual premium that does not rise over the duration of the policy. Whole life insurance is also referred to as "ordinary" or "straight" life insurance.

Will—A legal document that declares a person's wishes concerning the disposition of property, the guardianship of his or her children, and the administration of the estate after his or her death.

Yield—In general, the yield is the amount of current income provided by an investment. For stocks, the yield is calculated by dividing the total of the annual dividends by the current price. For bonds, the yield is calculated by dividing the annual interest by the current price. The yield is distinguished from the return, which includes price appreciation or depreciation.

Zero-Coupon Bond—This type of bonds makes no periodic interest payments but instead is sold at a steep discount from its face value. Bondholders receive the face value of their bonds when the bonds mature.

Reference Section

Put not your trust in money, but put your money in trust.
—*Oliver Wendell Holmes*

Chatzky, Jean. *You Don't Have To Be Rich*. New York, NY: Penguin, 2003.

Dent, Harry. *The Roaring 2000s*. New York, NY: Touchstone, 1998.

Hagstrom, Robert, Jr. *The Warren Buffet Way*. New York, NY: John Wiley & Sons, 1995.

Needleman, Jacob. *Money and the Meaning of Life*. New York, NY: Doubleday, 1991.

Tyson, Eric. *Personal Finance for Dummies*. Hoboken, NJ: Wiley Publishing, 2001.

Warren, Elizabeth and Tyagi Warren, Amelia. *The Two Income Trap: Why Middle-Class Mothers & Fathers Are Going Broke*. New York, NY: Perseus, 2003.

Resources

Money doesn't change men, it merely unmasks them.
If a man is naturally selfish or arrogant or greedy,
money will bring that out.—Henry Ford

Cash Management:
U.S. Department of the Treasury
Information about investing in Treasury bills, notes, and bonds.
202.874.4000
www.ustreas.gov

Comptroller of the Currency, Consumer Activities Division
Deals with consumer complaints and enforces regulations at
national banks—those with "National" or "N.A." in their names.
202.874.5000
www.occ.treas.gov

Federal Deposit Insurance Corporation, Office of Consumer Affairs
Answers questions on federal deposit insurance at banks,
thrifts, and savings and loans.
800.934.3342
www.fdic.gov

College Funding:
Federal Student Aid Information Center
An overview website for financial aid planning.
800.433.3243

Federal Student Aid
Free financial aid applications.
www.fafsa.gov

Credit Reporting Agencies:
Equifax
800.685.1111
www.equifax.com

Experian (formerly TRW)
888.397.3742
www.experian.com

TransUnion
800.632.1765
www.transunion.com

Estate Planning:
American Bar Association
The trade association for lawyers and can refer you to local members.
312.988.5000
www.abanet.org

Investment Planning:
> The Value Line Investment Survey
> Reviews over 1,700 stocks and rates them for risk potential and timely investing using a computer model based on the issuing company's earnings momentum.
> 800.833.0046
> *www.valueline.com*

> Morningstar Mutual Funds
> Offers comprehensive coverage on more than 7,000 mutual funds. Its five-star rating system measures both risk and return.
> 800.876.5005
> *www.morningstar.net*

> Standard & Poor's
> Has been rating bond issues since 1923, available in public libraries.
> 212.438.2000
> *www.standardandpoors.com*

> Moody's Investor Services
> Began rating bond issues in 1904, available in public libraries.
> 212.553.0377
> *www.moodys.com*

> National Association of Securities Dealers
> The regulating body for securities industry and can provide information about members' experience and disclose any disciplinary actions.
> 800.289.999
> *www.nasd.com*

Securities and Exchange Commission
Listing of registered financial professional advisors. Also
considers complaints about brokers, stock exchanges, and
corporate issuers of stocks and bonds.
202.942.7040
www.sec.gov

American Association of Individual Investors
Provides consumer education on investments.
800.428.2244
www.aaii.org

Miscellaneous:
Living to be 100
A unique website that allows you to estimate your life span.
www.livingto100.com

Dr. Ken Dychtwald
A leader in studying the effects and trends of aging adults.
www.agewave.com

Yahoo Financial
Website with easy-to-understand information and plenty of links.
www.yahoo.finance.com

"Personal Finance for Dummies" by Eric Tyson, M.B.A.
Written in simple everyday terms that discusses many
financial topics.
www.dummies.com

Periodicals:
Barron's
A weekly newspaper that reviews the investment markets.
800.568.7625
www.barrons.com

Business Week
Covers news developments on corporations, the economy,
and finance.
800.635.1200
www.businessweek.com

Forbes
Published bi-weekly focusing on large companies, money
and investing.
800.888.9896
www.forbes.com

Kiplinger's Personal Finance Magazine
Focuses on mutual fund investing, tax planning, retirement
planning, and other consumer issues.
800.544.0155
www.kiplinger.com

Money
Published monthly,concentrating on mutual funds and
money management features.
800.633.9970
www.money.com

The Wall Street Journal
The most widely read financial paper in the country.
800.568.7625
www.wsj.com

Retirement Planning:
American Association of Retired Persons
Offers member services; including insurance, pharmacy,
and travel.
202.434.2277
www.aarp.org

Social Security Administration
Can answer questions about your benefits.
800.772.1213
www.ssa.gov

Older Women's League
Advocacy group for women over 40.
202.783.6686

Risk Management
A.M. Best Company
The oldest and largest insurance company rating service.
908.439.2200
www.ambest.com

Standard & Poor's
Rates insurance company's claims-paying ability.
212.439.2000
www.standardandandpoors.com

Moody's Investor Services
Rates insurance companies, assigning them a letter grade
from Aaa for exceptional to C for lowest.
212.553.0377
www.moodys.com

National Insurance Consumer Help Line
Provides general information on life, home, health, and
auto insurance.
800.942.4242

American Council of Life Insurance
Provides publications on life insurance and annuities.
202.624.2000
www.acli.com

National Association of Insurance Commissioners
Offers links to each state's department of insurance.
www.naic.org

Tax Planning:
Internal Revenue Service
A toll-free help line to answer tax questions.
800.829.1040
www.irs.gov

American Institute of Certified Public Accountants (AICPA)
1211 Avenue of the Americas
New York, NY 10036
888.999.9256
www.cpapfs.org

About the Author

Pat Vitucci:

I was always interested in financial services. After graduation from Monmouth University in New Jersey, I accepted a position at a large financial insurance company where I worked in financial management for five years. I then worked as a financial analyst for another large Wall Street based financial services company, and then accepted an opportunity to manage a large subsidiary for them on the West Coast. My family and I moved to California and became acclimated to the area and pleasant climate.

When I decided to leave the company in the early 1990s, I established my own financial practice specializing in a broad array of investment management and financial advisory concepts. One of my primary principles is to focus on an *active* review of my clients' assets relative to current market conditions. Since my firm's inception, we have emphasized active asset allocation and disciplined diversification for our clients.

Our initial financial interview begins with an in-depth evaluation of the client's current financial situation. Once we have established the client's objectives, we'll focus on their specific goals. With today's ever changing economic conditions and market volatility, we invest our client's portfolio consistent with the client's tolerance for risk. Our staff is composed of a diverse and dedicated team of professionals who offer a committed and caring work ethic. Our securities are offered through AIG SunAmerica Securities, Inc, which has over 2200 licensed professionals nationwide. Our staff members have spent many years working closely with clients to assist them in meeting their financial objectives and goals. All of the securities are cleared through Pershing, a division of Donaldson, Lufkin & Jenrette.

At the beginning of this new century, managed assets in a volatile market has certainly been the defining challenge in managing our clients' portfolios. Significant rise in the stock markets during the 1990s, followed by a dramatic decline in the early 2000s, has been a vivid lesson that diversification and periodic reviews of a portfolio with active deployment is essential.

We also believe that asset allocation and risk profiles of the individual, or couple, changes over time. Thus, retirement plans, college funding plans, tax strategies, and estate planning should be top priorities for constant evaluation and adjustments.

Many people regard their financial choices as complex and confusing, plus they are too busy with their career and family life demands to remain focused on their financial life. One consideration is to outsource that function to a full-time team of financial professionals. This book is designed to assist the busy lay person and to help them with ways to keep their finger on the pulse of their investments.

Pat is the daily financial commentator on KABL and KFIA radio stations. He is also featured on the KTVU Noon News. Both radio and TV features are broadcast daily in the greater San Francisco Bay Area. Pat is also a frequent guest speaker at civic, industry association, and church groups, presenting salient financial commentary.